I0818246

ethikundgesellschaft

edited by

Volume 3

Torsten Meireis | Rolf Schieder [eds.]

Religion and Democracy

Studies in Public Theology

The Deutsche Nationalbibliothek lists this publication in the Deutsche Nationalbibliografie; detailed bibliographic data are available on the Internet at http://dnb.d-nb.de

ISBN 978-3-8487-4135-9 (Print)
978-3-8452-8444-6 (ePDF)

British Library Cataloguing-in-Publication Data
A catalogue record for this book is available from the British Library.

ISBN 978-3-8487-4135-9 (Print)
978-3-8452-8444-6 (ePDF)

Library of Congress Cataloging-in-Publication Data
Meireis, Torsten / Schieder, Rolf
Religion and Democracy
Studies in Public Theology
Torsten Meireis / Rolf Schieder (eds.)
181 p.
Includes bibliographic references.

ISBN 978-3-8487-4135-9 (Print)
978-3-8452-8444-6 (ePDF)

1. Edition 2017

Preface

This book is the product of a collective effort. We thank all the members of the newly founded Berlin Institute for Public Theology who agreed to contribute even before the official opening, who did so in a very cooperative spirit, never grumbling over extremely short deadlines and a strict editorial regime. We also thank Bettina Schön who did a tremendous job of layouting and editing, Mitch Cohen and Dr. Volker Manz who provided translation and English lecturing services, Beate Bernstein and Sonja Schmitt of the Nomos publishing house who took good care of our enterprise, the editors of Ethik und Gesellschaft who agreed to publish our book in their series and the EKD who supported this publication with a generous subsidy.

Torsten Meireis | Rolf Schieder

Table of Contents

Religion and Democracy: Tasks

Introduction:
Democracy, Religion and Public Theology

“Democracy isn’t dead, it just smells funny.” A variation of a quip by Frank Zappa on jazz (1974) sums up current experience with democracy. Even though a majority of countries in the world professes to some sort of democratic government (Campbell 2008), change is underfoot (EIU 2016). In Europe, democratically elected governments in Hungary and Poland are seriously limiting civil rights, in France, the Netherlands, in Sweden and Germany right-wing extremist political groups are gaining support. In Turkey, formerly seen as one of the most stable democracies in the Muslim world, Recep Tayyip Erdogan is effecting a change towards a more authoritarian system, and in the USA, the president himself is deemed a ‘threat to democracy’ (Levitsky/Ziblatt 2016), in South Africa, a corrupt government is causing turmoil, in the Philippines, an elected ruler openly voices contempt for human rights – the list of signs for a deterioration could be extended (Foa/Mounk 2016, 2017). Provided that liberal democracy, understood as a regime that combines free and fair elections, the citizens’ participation in politics, the protection of human rights of all inhabitants and a rule of Law (Diamond 1999, 1-19) qualifies as a highly desirable form of government, it seems worthwhile to look for ways of reviving and strengthening democracy.

Doubtlessly, religion is of some importance in that regard. This holds especially true if we take a historical perspective. While some types of reformed Protestantism were actually supportive of the emergence of democratic structures, other denominations, such as Lutherans or Roman Catholic Christians had a harder time accepting democracy (Graf 2014), and some, like Russian Orthodoxy, do so still. Similar findings can be presented for other religions (Diamond/Plattner 2005). And even though empirical evidence seems to suggest a special affinity of Christianity and democracy (Werkner/Liedhegener 2009), it’s hard to say whether this is due to historical circumstance or to an intrinsic necessity. In political theory, the question whether a democratic state needs to draw on religious resources is debated (Böckenförde 1991, Stein 2007, Anselm 2015). However, in the face of a decline of public support of democracy, the question in what way religion may support democratic government doesn’t seem too far-fetched.

This holds especially true in a public theological perspective. Public theology may be defined as an effort to explore and critically reflect on the public impact of a polyphonic religious discourse and the religious dimension of public discourse, while thus furthering the debates connected to such discourse. As public theology presupposes a public sphere where civil liberties hold and open debate is possible, it is therefore strongly connected to democratic forms of government. Public theology seeks to serve democratic societies which are pluralistic in world-view, providing research and expertise concerning the relationship of religious and secular world-views to the public sphere. As public theology denotes an effort of reflection, it is varied in itself – which also applies to its origins, as public theology sprang up in many different contexts. In the USA, it emerged as a historical label to characterize the impact of important Christian intellectuals like Reinhold Niebuhr (Marty 1974a, b) and quickly grew into a category to describe the public expressions of religious communities (Thiemann 1991), or the contribution of theology in regard to academy, religious community and society (Tracy 1975). Other approaches have tried to understand it as synonymous to political theology (Stackhouse 2000-2007) or connect its origins to civil religion (Breitenberg 2003). In South African discourse, the term was taken up when the dictatorial apartheid regime was supplanted by democratic government. Public theology then was introduced as successor concept for liberation theology which was directed against an oppressive regime, even though this is still contested (de Villiers 2013, Smit 2013, Maluleke 2011). In a pluralist and democratic society, liberation from economic or cultural distress may still be an issue, but cannot be effected through action against one identifiable agency of domination. In Germany, the concept cropped up as an alternative label for the efforts to understand theology as a critical instrument against social inequality and political domination which Johann Baptist Metz or Dorothee Sölle had called 'political theology', as that term had already been taken by Carl Schmitt's decisionist political thinking paving the way to Nazism and had roots in antiquity, where it signified a theology legitimizing the rulers in power (Maier 1970). It then developed into a term to signify social and societal critique (Huber 1999). Currently, the term 'public theology' describes a form of discourse rather than one theological position and unites theologians from different contexts in a global network designed to serve international exchange on the public impact of a polyphonic religious discourse and the significance of religious topics for public discourse.

As public theology carries a strong affinity to democracy, a critical analysis of how religions may beware of hindering and succeed in furthering democratic forms of government seems appropriate.

This book then tries just that in presenting essays from different public theological perspectives. It aims at an interdisciplinary, ecumenical and interreligious assessment of how religion may further democracy. All texts have been contributed by members of the newly founded Berlin Institute for Public Theology who consent to the necessity of a public theological effort, especially in regard to the question of democracy, but debate on what this effort needs to consist in. Of course, it's only the start of a discussion that needs to be continued.

The book consists of three sections: A first section tries to identify challenges and resources in the relationship of religion and democracy. A second part reflects on the frameworks of that relationship, and a third section tries to identify examples of tasks that need to be shouldered.

A first chapter is concerned with present-day challenges to democracy and resources in a public-theological view, looking especially at the role of religion. *Torsten Meireis* explores current developments in Europe and the US that may be understood as post-democratic: the rise of nationalist and xenophobic movements that claim popular support but aim at severely cutting into those civil rights usually associated with democratic government. From a Protestant Christian theological perspective, he then outlines the ambivalent picture in Protestantism. He names doctrinal and empirical problems concerning religion and democracy and maps resources for a sustainment of democracy Protestantism has to offer.

Rolf Schieder tackles the challenge presented by accusations of blasphemy to the central democratic right to freedom of expression. After characterizing blasphemy theologically as a relationship between the faithful and the deity, he argues politically for a freedom of religion that implies an abolition of legislation on blasphemy. In a survey of current French and German developments he shows that in modern nation-states, anti-blasphemy laws are used to preserve a civil-religious national consensus rather than to defend a deity or its worshippers. In a Christian perspective, he then contends that a God who gave himself over to public shaming on the cross won't be interested in a preservation of divine honor.

In a second section, we'll take a step back to explore the frameworks in the relationship of religions and democracy from different angles. *Andreas Feldtkeller* takes a religious studies-perspective: in discerning a historically informed typology of social formations of religion, he asserts that there is no typical political or social expression of religion as such. Rather, a specific religion's political impact results from the combination of doctrines and social formations in a given societal frame. Therefore, public theology needs to be aware of the fact that any political religious statement will be understood in the "context of the community's social body-language". A public theology trying to strengthen a human rights approach, for instance, in relying on a Christian concept of universal neighborly love constantly has to reflect critically on how doctrinal aspects of faith are embodied in the respective community's social formations and actions and the 'civil religion' legitimizing current structures of power. From a cultural studies point of view, *Marcia Pally* expounds on an anthropological thesis. Humans are characterized, she asserts, by a structure of distinction-amid-relation best expressed by the biblical covenantal tradition, discernible in all abrahamic religions, but explored in depth by Christian reformed thinkers. As that idea has been formative for the emergence of democracy in the United States of America, Pally claims that it also holds promise for present politics, as a covenantal worldview and mindset takes into account the respective opponents' view as a respectable one. In an overview of the debates on democracy in the Muslim world, *Mouez Khalfaoui* brings an Islamic theological view to the fore. After a description of the reception of democratic ideas in 19th century Islamic theology, he goes on to show how democracy became an exclusive issue for Western-trained elites and only in recent times shifted towards a public recognition. Using the example of the Iranian revolution Khalfaoui then argues that – the later development of the theocratic regime nonwithstanding – democracy started to become a threat to authoritarian governments in the Islamic world, especially in the Arab spring of 2011, where Muslim groups were among the promoters of democracy. Regarding the relationship of Muslim faith and democracy in the western world, Khalfaoui then proposes to focus on everyday Muslim life rather than relying on the doctrinal claims of ultraconservative minority groups to grasp Muslim perspectives on democracy. In an ethical perspective, Roman Catholic theologian *Matthias Möhring-Hesse* explores the relationship of religion and politics in regard to democratic deliberation. As modernity brought about a separation of politics and faith systems during which the latter became 'religion', 'ultimate' questions were removed from the area of politics, which is – in a democratic system – based on common deliberations. For the faithful, politics will probably be seen as one field of many where they practice their faith. For others, however, their faith is neither necessarily visible nor of argumentative value in the course of political deliberation, since religious arguments are by nature only valid in the community that shares them. For that reason, religious citizens need to make themselves understood in a political process, where a common normative language usually needs to be found: that may involve the use of religious language, but necessarily also the expression in arguments that citizens who do not share those views may understand. As believers theologically take up and interpret issues that they find in their everyday world, secular meaning precedes religious interpretation.

A third section then looks at different tasks necessary to strengthen democracy in a public theological perspective that range from a critical look at the responsibility discourse to problems of empowerment and institutional questions.

In a Christian theological perspective interested in strengthening the position of the least privileged, *Florian Höhne* scrutinizes the responsibility discourse stressing the individual's democratic responsibility in media-related public communication. After presenting media-ethical positions that attribute a high responsibility to the public – understood as consisting of individual 'prosumers' – he points to the ambivalence of responsibility-talk that doesn't take capability into the account and thus holding the relatively powerless to the same responsibility as the comparatively powerful. Concluding, he suggests to sharpen the media responsibility discourse by discerning who responsibility may be attributed to in which regard, by furthering public discourse about the appropriate attribution of responsibility and by remembering the democratic roots of the responsibility talk, i.e. to hold the powerful responsible. On a corresponding note, *Clemens Wustmans* takes a critical look at the exclusive nature of theological language, measuring public theology at its claims to further general participation. He then goes on to expound the concept of plain language as part of the capabilities approach that needs to be implemented in public theological debates, too – even though tensions remain, as reduction in complexity cannot be avoided when using the plain language concept.

The concluding texts look at institutional contributions of public theology to democracy. In that vein, *Christine Schliesser* argues for a strengthening of theological arguments in institutionalized public discourse, whereas *Eva Harasta* pleads for a stronger awareness of the public sphere in church organizations. *Schliesser* looks into the ongoing political practice of ethics councils to clarify the role and possible contribution of public theology to democratic institutions. Based on empirical research, she describes the setting of ethics councils of Germany and Switzerland, then explores the role of theology in those institutions by comparing member statements. As the results reveal a certain vagueness regarding the theological background of normative arguments, Schliesser goes on to suggest a Christian theological interpretation of public theology based on the doctrine of the munus triplex of Christ to heighten the sensibility for theological argumentation in democratic contexts and its accountability. *Harasta*, subscribing to Bedford-Strohm's characterization of public theology as liberation theology for democratic societies, presents the current debate in the Lutheran World Federation as a case-study for the entanglement of public theological reflection between academia, religious community's superstructure and the nation state, advocating a stronger awareness of the public sphere in such religious institutions.

As public theology stands for a self-critical look at religion, but also the research in what religion has to offer in regard to democratic society, this book tries to contribute to a critical albeit constructive inside perspective on religion and democracy. As such, we at the Berlin Institute for Public Theology understand it as an invitation to further critical discourse.

Berlin, Spring 2017

Torsten Meireis
Rolf Schieder

References

Anselm, Reiner (2015): Politische Ethik, in: Wolfgang Huber, Torsten Meireis, Hans-Richard Reuter (eds.), *Handbuch der Evangelischen Ethik*, München: Beck, 195-263.

Böckenförde, Ernst-Wolfang (1991): Die Entstehung des Staates als Vorgang der Säkularisation, in: E.-W. Böckenförde, *Recht, Staat, Freiheit. Studien zur Rechtsphilosophie, Staatstheorie und Verfassungsgeschichte*, Frankfurt am Main: Suhrkamp, 92-114.

Breitenberg, E. Harold (2003): To tell the Truth. Would the Real Public Theology Please Stand up? *Journal of the Society of Christian Ethics*, 23/2 2003, 55-96.

Campbell, David F.J. (2008): *The Basic Concept for the Democracy Ranking of the Quality of Democracy*. Vienna: Democracy Ranking.

Diamond, Larry (1999): *Developing Democracy: Toward Consolidation*, Baltimore: Johns Hopkins University Press.

Diamond, Larry, Plattner, Harold, Costopuoulos, Philipp J. (eds.) (2005): *World Religions and Democracy*, Baltimore: Johns Hopkins University Press.

EIU (The Economist Intelligence Unit) (2016): *Democracy Index 2016. Revenge of the 'Deplorables'*, A Report by The Economist Intelligence Unit, London.

Foa, Roberto Steven, Munk, Yascha (2016): The Democratic Disconnect, *Journal of Democracy* Vol. 27, Number 3 July 2016, 5-17.

Foa, Roberto Steven, Munk, Yascha (2017): The Signs of Deconsolidation, *Journal of Democracy* Vol. 28, Number 1 January 2017, 5-15.

Graf, Friedrich-Wilhelm (2014), *Götter global. Wie die Welt zum Supermarkt der Religionen wird*, München: Beck.

Huber, Wolfgang (1999): *Kirche in der Zeitenwende*. Gütersloh: Gütersloher Verlag.

Levitsky, Steven, Ziblatt, Daniel (2016): Is Donald Trump a Threat to Democracy? *The New York Times*, Dec. 16th, 2016, https://www.nytimes.com/2016/12/16/opinion/sunday/is-donald-trump-a-threat-to-democracy.html (accessed April 13th, 2017).

Maier, Hans (1970): Kritik der Politischen Theologie, in: Hans Maier, *Politische Religionen*, Gesammelte Aufsätze Bd. 2, Regensburg 2007, 15-74 (Date of original publication: 1970).

Maluleke, Tinyiko Sam (2011): *Reflections and Resources. The Elusive Public of Public Theology*:

A Response to William Storrar, *International Journal of Public Theology* 5 (2011), 79–89.

Marty, Martin E.: Two Kinds of Two Kinds of Civil Religion, in: Russell E. Richey/ Donald G. Jones (eds.): *American Civil Religion* (= A Harper forum book), New York: Harper & Row, 139–157.

Marty, Martin E. (1974): Public Theology: Reinhold Niebuhr and the American Experience, *The Journal of Religion*, 54/4 1974b, 332-359.

Smit, Dirk J. (2013): The Paradigm of Public Theology - Origins and Development, in: Bedford-Strohm, Heinrich, Höhne, Florian, Reitmeier, Tobias (eds.), *Contextuality and Intercontextuality in Public Theology*. Proceedings from the Bamberg Conference 23.-25.06.2011, Münster: Lit, 11-24.

Stackhouse, Max (ed.) (2000-2007), *God and Globalization*, Vol. 1-4, Harrisburg/New York: Continuum.

Stein, Tine (2007): *Himmlische Quellen und irdisches Recht. Religiöse Voraussetzungen des freiheitlichen Verfassungsstaates*, Frankfurt, New York: Campus.

Thiemann, Ronald F. (1991), *Constructing a Public Theology*. Westminster.

Tracy, David (1975): Theology as Public Discourse, in: *Christian Century* 92, 1975, 280-284.

Villiers, Etienne de (2013), Public Theology in the South African Context, *Theologia Viatorum* Vol. 37/1 2013, http://citeseerx.ist.psu.edu/viewdoc/download doi=10.1.1.1006.9111&rep=rep1&type=pdf (accessed April 3rd 2017).

Werkner, Ines-Jacqueline, Liedhegener, Antonius (2009): Einleitung: Von "Demokratie und Religion" zu "Religionen und Demokratie", in: I-J. Werkner, A. Liedhegener (ed.): *Religionen und Demokratie. Beiträge zu Genese, Geltung und Wirkung eines aktuellen politischen Spannungsfeldes*, Wiesbaden: Verlag für Sozialwissenschaften, 9-14.

Zappa, Frank (1974): BeBop Tango (of the Old Jazzmen's Church), *Album Roxy and Elsewhere*, DiscReet Records.

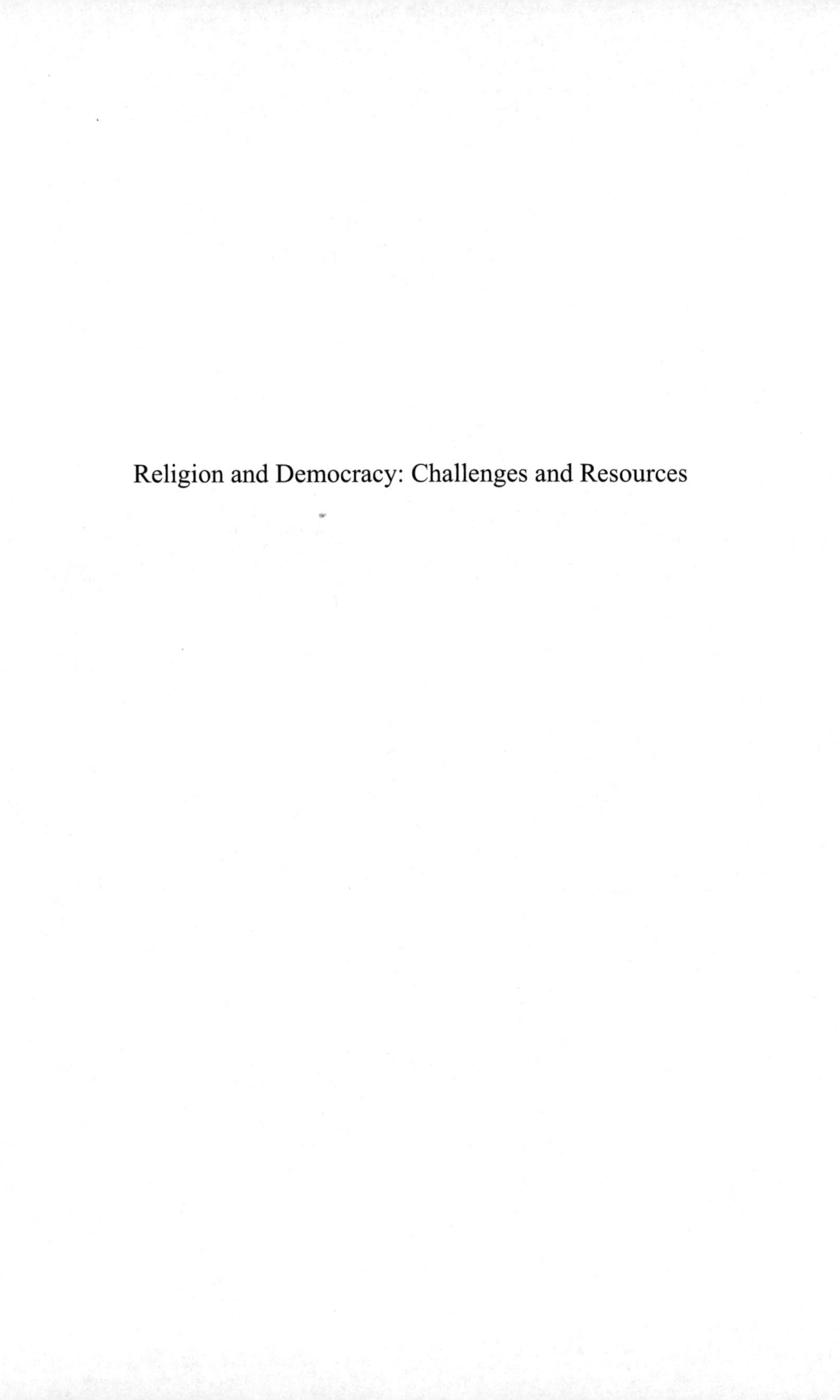

Religion and Democracy: Challenges and Resources

Public Theology in a Post-democratic Age?
Perspectives from a European Context

Torsten Meireis

The end of democracy as we know it?

The idea of democracy seems to have faded of late. It didn't need the election of Donald Trump as 45th president of the United States of America, the spectacular successes of ultra-right-wing Marine Le Pen in France or AfD's notorious Bjoern Hoecke in Germany to show that there is deep and wide-spread discontent among voters directed against the so-called established parties and candidates which apparently can be readily channeled into nationalist, xenophobic or outright anti-democratic views. And even though respective leaders don't seem overly religious, religion seems to be involved in such issues: Le Pen attacked her rival to the presidency, Francois Fillon, on accounts of his profession to the Christian faith in matters of social security. She claimed that Fillon had opportunistically violated the French concept of laïcité, the strict separation of faith and state (Valeurs actuelles 2017). Le Pen, on the other hand, had no qualms about assuring Lebanon's Maronite Christian leader Roger Eddé that she would defend eastern Christians, "since blood ties were the closest of all." (Haddad 2017) Donald Trump, even though apparently no church member anymore (Prömpers 2017; Burke 2016), drew voters especially from the white, evangelical born-again Christians across denominations (81 %), the Protestants (58 %) and the white Catholic side (60 %) (Smith & Martinez 2016). The Protestant Church in Saxony, Germany, is openly divided on the question about ministry of AfD and Pegida-followers (Hähnig 2016; Reinhard 2016; Richter 2017).

Political affinities of religious devotees, the role of religions in civil society and the state, and the relationship of religion and democracy all touch on the very core of what may be called public theology (Hoehne & van Oorschot 2015). By "public theology" I understand first and foremost an academic effort of reflection aimed at questions concerning the religious dimension of public debates and the public dimension of religious debates (Meireis 2013a). As a theological effort, it originates from the inside of religious worldviews rather than from an outside point of view. Its public focus implies an academic scrutiny of public discussion as well as the involvement in such debates. Although public theology developed in quite different contexts and varieties of Protestant Christian thought, it is by no means limited to a Protestant or even Christian stance. As it always implies the reflection on one's own context and situation of knowledge, however, the respective religious perspective needs to be identified: mine is Protestant Christian of a rather reformed variety and European.

In the following paper I'd like to take you with me on a little journey in the course of which we will first of all take a view at evidence that points to a dramatic loss in democratic substance in not only newly converted but allegedly traditionally stable democratic countries that has been labelled by the term of post-democracy (Crouch 2004). I will present a *European* view including some analytic ideas, although to me the problem seems to have encompassed all of what is metaphorically called 'the West', paralleling some developments in what may be called 'young democracies' in the global east and south. The second stop on our journey will be dedicated to a short look at the challenges this development presents for public theology in a Protestant Christian perspective empirically as well as doctrinally and the resources we might rely on to meet those challenges. Ultimately I hope to arrive at an outlook concerning measures to be taken by protagonists of public theology in religious communities, academy and society at large.

1. A Post-democratic age?

1.1 The situation

First of all I'd like to sketch a picture of what I see as evidence for a loss in democratic substance. For the sake of not overstretching the argument, I'll refrain here from using Barber's notions of Strong Democracy (Barber 1984) or Habermas' deliberative theory (Habermas 1992) but will use a normative definition that is less demanding. By democracy I understand a governance that's usually based on a minority-sensitive idea of a nonviolently changing majority rule usually operated by some sort of representative mechanism and presupposing political freedoms and an active civil society where problem descriptions are generated to be fed into the policy cycle. Three normative concepts, however, are essential: the idea of general civic participation and majority rule protected from autocracies by instruments like the checks and balances system (1), the possibility of nonviolent change (2) and the concept of protecting minorities from disenfranchisement or a general denial of rights through majorities (3) – this is what I would call the substance of democracy. However, currently exactly that substance is threatened all over the world.

All across Europe, there has been a dwindling in voting participation, paralleling the notoriously low numbers in US-American elections. This proves especially true in the case of the European Parliament, where participation dropped dramatically from a 62% in 1979 to 43% in 2014 (Statista 2016a), but it's also visible in countries like Germany (Statista 2016b), where overall numbers have lowered to around 71%, in France, where numbers have dropped from 70–80% in the fifties, sixties and seventies to around 55% in 2012, in the United Kingdom, where numbers used to be high in the 70s and 80s now are at 66% in 2015, but also in young democracies like Poland, where participation dropped from around 60% since the democratic change down to around 50% today, or Hungary, where it declined from numbers high in the sixties down to 61% (IDEA 2017a). Of course, reasons are various and numerous, but still a tendency is clearly visible – in US presidential elections voting participation has gone down from 95% in 1964 to 66% in 2012, with parliamentary votes turnout considerably lower (from almost 90% in 1968 to 42.5% in 2014) (IDEA 2017b). Just for comparison: In the Republic of South Africa, voter turnout has gone down from around 87% in 1994 to 73.5% in 2014 (IDEA 2017c).

Not only in the German speaking world, a public distrust in the press and politics proper has arisen in the last five years. Especially right-wing populists accuse the media of being in league with an elitist government and have taken up an old Nazi propaganda slogan describing the media as "lying press", "Lügenpresse" (Haller 2015), thus avoiding debate and discourse necessary for a functioning civil society. In the US, Donald Trump openly claims that the media systematically fabricate fake news: "We are not going to let the fake news tell us what to do, how to live and what to believe," he said. "We are free, independent people and we will make our own choices." (Jacobs 2017) At the same time, he spreads information relying on dubitable sources which often prove wrong (Maheshwari 2017).

Instead of an open issue-oriented discourse in civil society we see a strong dramatization and personalization of politics, where individual character traits or even looks are considered more decisive then policies – if we look at Clinton vs. Trump, Johnson and Farage vs. Cameron or Obama vs. Putin, the images created are even more important than people's actual decisions. The fact that Boris Johnson has knowingly spread factually false information about Britain's dues to the EU during the Brexit campaign (Staufenberg 2016) did not hamper his way to Great Britain's foreign ministry in any way.

Furthermore, an intensive renationalization of policies and polities is visible implying a retraction of democratic mechanisms to govern international relations – paradoxically in the name of democracy. Not only have border controls been reintensified even in traditionally open countries like Sweden or Denmark (AFP 2016) and even more so in freshly democratic countries like Hungary or the Czech Republic in the course of what was named the "refugee crisis" (and the term was not applied to the situation of the refugees from civil strife in Syria or Afghanistan but to that of the more or less affluent European countries). Anti-European movements became more and more popular, not only in the UK, where Nigel Farage's United Kingdom Independence Party has successfully led a campaign to vote for a "Brexit", but also in the Netherlands (Geert Wilders' "Partij voor de Vrijheid"), in France (FN) or in Germany (AfD). A certain anticlimax is reached in traditionally democratic Switzerland, where the most popular and successful party, the SVP, has announced to bring in an "initiative for self-governance" that ultimately aims at renouncing the European Convention on Human Rights to unfetter majority rule in Switzerland (Brotschi 2016). Interestingly, one of the reasons given for opting out of the EU is its democratic deficit in terms of transparency and representation – however, international relations only governed by the particular interests of nation state's governments tend to be anarchic rather than democratic.

Finally, all across Europe and in the US, too, extremist positions and movements, most of them right-wing populists, gain increasing influence on governments with the clear intention of cracking down on civil liberties, participation rights and open discourse in civil society essential even to normatively 'thin' versions of democracy. There is the Swiss SVP already mentioned, which has successfully initiated a referendum to amend the Swiss constitution with a ban on minarets (Swiss Constitution Art. 72,3), blatantly neglecting religious freedom professed in the same document (Swiss Constitution Art. 15). Hungary's Victor Orbán has passed a new constitution in 2011, effectively privileging ethnic Magyars against, for instance, Hungarian Roma (Salzborn 2015). Orbán, professing to make Hungary an illiberal state, is using governmental power to reserve Budapest's central places during national holidays for his own governmental party, Fidesz, effectively keeping out the opposition (Verseck 2015; Ritterband 2012). In close alliance Poland's Prime Minister Beata Szydlo, President Andrzej Duda and party leader and strongman Jarozlav

Kaczynski have effectively crippled Poland's supreme court to ease PiS' authoritarian rule (Winterbauer 2016). The attempt to ban any abortion and the illiberal tendencies have already led to large protest demonstrations (Wirtschaftswoche 2016). We can skip further stories from Romania, Bulgaria or Russia, because traditional "Western" states also experience severe challenges to democracy. In Germany, the newly founded "Alternative for Germany" which may be understood as the political arm of the xeno- and islamophobic Pegida movement and which also takes a strong populist stance, demonizing political elites, is entering local parliaments. In France, the ultra-right wing "Front National" has swept the city halls in 2015 regional elections, becoming the strongest faction with around 30% of the votes (Wernicke 2015). In Finland, the "Perussuomalaiset", the right wing populist "Finns Party" (formerly "Party of the True Finns"), voting against Europe, migration and Swedish as an obligatory language in school, have become part of the government (Sundberg 2015). In Sweden, the Sverigedemokraterna, the "Swedish Democrats", opting against migration, Europe and having developed out of openly racist movements, have entered parliament with as much as 12% of the vote and get as much as 17.5% in current polls (The Local 2016). Similar tendencies are to be noted in Italy (Lega Nord), in Greece (Chrysio Augio), in the Netherlands (PvV), in Belgium (Flemish Block), in Austria (FPÖ) and in other countries.

1.2 Analysis

One of the most influential analyses of the processes involved has been developed by Colin Crouch, who has coined the term post-democracy. His theory combines older insights presented by Schumpeter's empirical theory of democracy (2003) (which already counted on a fabricated public opinion) with a historical thesis and presupposes a normative basis close to Barber's and Habermas' ideas. To Crouch, modern democracies suffer from three ailments. First of all, the identity of class or religious interests and political parties that had developed in the struggles of the 19th century is fading, and although Crouch contends that there are still classes, they didn't develop political identities – with one exception. Crouch sees that exception in major shareholders and business executives who had an economic and political theory he calls neoliberalism and effectively struggled for a concurrent organization of transnational and national economic relations called globalization. Secondly Crouch contends that, due to the fading and outdated identities of political parties, political leaders found it more and more difficult to access voters through the rank and file of their parties because both groups are increasingly different. For that reason, they associated firstly with counseling firms and spin doctors, allowing to address the voters directly, albeit not with the tedious and time-consuming process of political programs and civil debate but with the toolbox of modern marketing. Secondly they mainly dealt with powerful economic agents, especially at the top of the hierarchy, who were better educated, had more power and opportunities and political ideas than the party rank and file – and were ready to finance the counseling firms deemed necessary to win elections. The third ailment of democracy is what Crouch sees as a politically engineered increasing powerlessness of the democratically organized nation state in the globalization process, having to do with the increasing connection of political and business leaders – the concomitant theory of neoliberalism then weakens and commercializes public wealth and goods distributed by the public hand, thus further estranging citizens from their own governments.

Crouch's analysis can be underpinned by critiques of representation and formal procedure in combination with a problematized liberal concern for formal freedom of choice as opposed to a substantial common good as brought forth by Adrian Pabst (2016). The argument contends that liberal democracies enhance individual and negative freedom, thereby privileging those who are able to effectively voice and promote their interests – those, however, who would profit most from substantial commons (public swimming pools and libraries, public housing and so on) tend to be those least able to effectively fight for them. If we add empirical insights into the phenomenon of structural group-related misanthropy (Heitmeyer 2007), we can also see that one of the main triggers for xenophobia and racism is the fear of imminent social descent especially in the middle strata of society, the blue collar people struck hardest by tertiarization and the threat of poverty (Hüpping & Reinecke 2007). This effect may be enhanced as a welfare state who in times of new public management and neoliberalism is becoming more and more harsh towards its needy clients seems to be opened up to people the less well-off understand as rivals and competitors who – in contrast to themselves – don't seem to have to work or accept degrading examinations to get support: And it's the refugees and immigrants who seem to unfairly get something for nothing, especially if some of them do actually pose a real threat (Nassehi 2015).

2. *Public theology from a Protestant European perspective: challenges and resources*

2.1 Challenges

How is public theology to deal with that development – and should it do so at all? The presupposition here is that public theology implies a certain affinity to democratic procedure, as it is closely linked to the modern idea of a civil society and the freedom of public expression it implies. However, Christian faith is not a political doctrine, it has thrived under various regimes and cannot be simply identified with a democratic political order.

If the first set of challenges for public theology is – in a way – doctrinal, it can be summed up in the notion that religion and politics are separate realms that are not to be entangled. The second set of challenges is of an institutional nature, having to do with the way most of the larger Protestant Churches in Europe are set up sociologically and in terms of organization. I will first explain those challenges and then try to deal with them by pointing out the doctrinal, institutional and social resources a public theology has to offer in response to post-democratic developments. But, challenges first.

2.1.1 Doctrinal challenges

Regarding Christianity as a whole, one could contend that Christendom has flourished under many regimes. In the view of protestant theologian Ernst Troeltsch, author of the seminal study on the social teachings of the Christian churches (1912), one of the reasons for that lies in Christian doctrine itself, which, to his mind, doesn't contain a political theory proper but accommodates to existing regimes. Its contribution consists in two aspects. The first aspect lies in the fact that Christian thought is essentially eschatological. As a result of his historical research, Troeltsch contended that the idea of the second coming of Christ usually implied that Christians could accept almost any political regime, as it was deemed temporary and of no lasting import. At the same time, Christians taught the infinite worth of the individual implied in Christ's teaching. To Troeltsch both aspects – the idea that Christians should accept existing political structures and the concept of the infinite worth of the person – imply that Christianity cannot be bound to a certain polity but is conservative and progressive (democratic) at the same time (Troeltsch 1904). If that holds true, the attempt to further democracy theologically might be futile, and the idea of a public theology might seem rather awkward.

Concerning Protestantism, especially the doctrine of two kingdoms and two regimes of God is noteworthy. According to Augustine's "De Civitate Dei", the world "civitas terrena" is a battle ground, whereas the heavenly kingdom, "civitas coelestis", manifests itself in Christians. The early mediaeval two swords doctrine then maintained that spiritual and worldly powers have different swords. On that basis, Luther (1523) developed his doctrine of the two regimes of God: in his worldly regime, God acts through the existing authorities and the sword to hinder sin from destroying the world, whereas in his spiritual regime God reigns through the word of Christ alone, leading men to salvation. In the course of history, the doctrine, originally devised to ban religious violence and foster a religious freedom based on the concept of God's sovereign will which may and cannot be harnessed by any church hierarchy, became a stepping stone of a compartmentalization of religion and politics. As regional authorities won domination of the Reformation churches, the doctrine was increasingly understood to simply legitimize existing authority; in its modern, post-enlightenment form it is interpreted as a legitimation of the secular state (Honecker 1990, 214–226). For those who hold that view, "public theology" is a contradictio in adiecto. Thus, the two kingdoms doctrine has been construed to condone two juxtaposed positions: in pre-modern times, it was counterintuitively misused to justify the ruler's religion to dominate the public square. In the course of the 19th and 20th century, it was then understood as a doctrinal basis to account for the claim that religious beliefs are indifferent to political questions.

Concomitant with the aforesaid views was the Lutheran tradition of a political authority that had to ensure the subjects' welfare, albeit in a very paternalistic way, whereas in reformed traditions the individual responsibility was stressed. In both traditions, an alleged difference between deserving and undeserving poor made for a very harsh treatment of the needy, who were usually seen as vice-ridden and whose structural affliction was usually ignored. Following that line, a protestant public theology arguing for a generous welfare state equipping all citizens with resources needed to ensure political participation might at least seem unusual (Meireis 2005).

Additionally, the church itself cannot easily be seen as a wholly democratic structure, since it may not be envisaged as a political organization solely originating in its members intentions and actions: for in a theological perspective, the church is instituted by God's revelation in Jesus Christ, thus aiming at salvation, not domination.

2.1.2 Institutional and social challenges

There are not only doctrinal but also empirically accessible challenges to a public theology fostering democracy. First of all, democratic procedures in existing churches and communities tend to be problematic affairs, too. Even though most Protestant Churches adhere to such procedures, more often than not, ministers enjoy undue influence in parish councils. Additionally, finding candidates for presbyters or elders is a tedious affair, and the voting turnout in parish elections is scanty. On the other hand, some clergy – especially bishops in some church organizations – are elected for lifetime, which is problematic in a democratic perspective (Pausch 2013).

Secondly, public impact of political statements by church bodies is dwindling. In the Swiss minaret debate, for instance, almost all the mainline Christian churches (and other religious communities) argued against a minaret ban. The SVP (Swiss People's Party), who initiated the referendum in favor of the minaret ban, however, claimed that banning minarets was the Christian thing to do for reasons of preserving the Christian heritage – and that argument, effectively amplified by the party's apparatus, almost neutralized the other votes (Tanner et al. 2009).

Thirdly, there is a strong social bias in Protestant Church membership, at least in the German speaking world. Church members are predominantly well educated, rather traditional and reasonably well off, even if scared of social descent (EKD 2007, 51). The poor usually do not belong, whereas the middle classes afraid of slipping into scarcity, however, do, and there is ongoing debate over the compatibility of church membership and membership in the right-wing AfD. If churches cannot ensure some sort of social equality and consequently equal political participation in their own organizations – how can they go public with alleged insights?

2.2 Resources

Of course, this is not the end of that story, because I will argue that there are quite vibrant doctrinal and social resources Protestant Christian public theology may muster to further democracy[1] – I would like to briefly outline three of each.

2.2.1 Doctrinal resources

Doctrinally, we have gone quite a way since the days of Ernst Troeltsch. There are, to my mind, at least three arguments to ponder. They all have to do with the reconsideration of doctrine in the face of historical experience and the reconsideration of history in the light of the word of God. First of all, the idea that Christian thought is easily compatible with any political regime whatsoever has been strongly contested by public theological thinkers (sans phrase) like Paul Tillich (1932), a student of Troeltsch's, Reinhold Niebuhr (1932), Dietrich Bonhoeffer (1934), Karl Barth (1946), by Rubem Alves (1969), Jürgen Moltmann (1970), Dorothee Sölle (1971), Desmond Tutu (1982) and others who represent a variety of political views. The historical reason is of course what has been seen as the failure of Christians to respond to political injustice, violence and oppression in the spirit of Christ, turning to the oppressed and speaking out against oppression: this failure has triggered not only repentance but also processes of learning and reconsidering scriptural and doctrinal evidence. One of the doctrinal reasons is a different attitude towards God's kingdom, which is now understood as God's ultimate promise relevant for the penultimate, as the fifth thesis of the Declaration of Barmen (1934) contends. The methodological reason for that change in attitude is that Troeltsch's historical relativism has been disputed, since that kind of relativism could only be held in the perspective of a position that could overlook all of human history, which of course none of us can. The truth in Troeltsch's claim, however, is the idea of epistemic self-limitation, or rather the insight into our own limits. If we refrain from claiming God's position, we must acknowledge epistemic limitations and accept other claims to truth. A political regime Christians can accept must, therefore, at least protect everybody's freedom to think and voice their respective world views, religious or not, in general but also in regard to political consequences.

---

1 This contention is non-exclusive, it doesn't imply that other public theologies such as Muslim or Jewish public theology couldn't muster such resources – but, of course, they will have to do so themselves.

Secondly, that type of self-limitation lets us see an affinity between the Christian view of the polity, policy and politics in its current primary figure, the nation state, and a democratic political order. As I've argued elsewhere (Meireis 2013b), we can use Karl Barth's (1946) version of the doctrine of the two regimes of God as an example here. Following the French political theorist Claude Lefort (1990), democracy can be described as a system where minorities are protected and political change is structurally enabled. This is ensured by keeping the function, the image and the place of the sovereign empty. While in the political doctrine of the Ancien Régime (or modern dictatorships, for that matter) the ruler embodies the people and by that imagery holds sovereignty in his person, representative democracy constitutes a difference: the alleged sovereign, the people, delegate their sovereignty, the representatives hold it only temporary and by proxy. So as Lefort contends, the place of the sovereign remains empty. The same is true for Barth's vision of the relationship between church and state. While Christians profess that Christ is head of church and state at the same time, that Christ is the true sovereign, they may not rule in Christ's stead because that would constitute an usurpation of God's position. For that reason, as far as politics are concerned, the place of the sovereign remains removed. Thus, Christians may act as citizens in the light of their respective convictions, but without any special authority – even amongst themselves (which is why Barth resented Christian parties), as the doctrine of the universal priesthood of the faithful contends. And they will have to fight any position trying to fill the place of the sovereign, anybody claiming to embody any given people – which amounts to something like a pluralistic and impartial state in questions of religions and worldviews.

Thirdly, the understanding of human dignity as God's gift, exemplified by God's dignifying humanity by the doubly universal address of man as God's image and steward and as a called beneficiary of Christ's redemption, implies two things (Meireis 2008, 344–379). First of all, the equality of human dignity makes it a matter of justice that there are equal participation rights in the formulation of those political rules that govern the feasible distribution of life chances. This holds true especially if we accept the perspective of the disenfranchised and oppressed as the most relevant in a Christian view. Secondly, the idea of being called into responsibility for one's neighbor requires investment into that calling. Both arguments strongly favor a generous welfare state, especially if we consider the close connection between such a welfare state and democratic empowerment – and indeed European Protestant theology has moved in that direction.

2.2.2 Institutional resources

But, of course, there are also institutional and social resources public theology in many parts of Europe may draw upon to further democracy. First of all, there is a stock of well-established democratic procedures in Protestant Churches – elected parish councils, synodal structures and so on – which is by now deeply ingrained, regardless of its shortcomings. Church hierarchy – spiritual or political – is as a rule rather frowned upon; churches for that reason provide social capital in the Putnam sense of the word (EKD 2014, 108–116).

Since the 19th century, a culture of public deliberation (intra and extra muros ecclesiae) has developed, slowly replacing claims of religious domination with a public theological reflection on the necessity of self-limitation sketched above (Anselm 2015). This is supported by academic endeavor and ministerial formation at universities. Theology placed at university has to keep in contact and discourse with all kinds of other scientific cultures, thus keeping alert to the multitude of world views and scientific normative positions (cf. Pannenberg 1973) and thus honing its skills of systematical and public theological reflection.

And of course the political and diaconal efforts in contexts like urban industrial mission, in political debates on the future of the welfare state or the empowerment of the less well-to-do in the framework of the aforementioned cultures of public deliberation form a resource to strengthen the basis of formal democracy (Meireis 2015).

3. Consequences for a public theology of the future

So, what can public theology do in a post-democratic age?

First of all, a public theology aiming at a reflexive discourse in a pluralist context keeping its limits in mind and insisting in word and deed on democratic structures and a religiously impartial state remains most important. Only if we take complaints and fears of those turning from democracy serious, we can support the claim that democracy is indeed the lesser evil as it carries the promise of universal access and participation in making the rules that govern the distribution of chances.

Secondly, the critical stance against the usurpation of sovereignty by the identification of one person, party or religion with the sovereign remains central to public theology, as I see it.

Thirdly, the social, ethical and political effort to further a generous welfare state giving people access to resources needed to put participation into practice is crucial. It has to be complemented by a self-critical view on church membership insofar as it mainly consists of the privileged – and by the development of procedures and practices pertaining to a more inclusive scenario.

Post-democracy, as I see it, is not fate but the unintended product of human interaction. As such, it is a phenomenon Karl Barth probably would have counted among the notorious lordless powers, which are real enough albeit ultimately empty. Hope against such powers comes from praying, enlightenment about their nature, from thinking, and patience, from actively waiting for God's kingdom. So let's pray, think and act.

References

AFP (2016): One of Europe's most open borders has just been closed, *AFP* 01/04/2016, http://www.thejournal.ie/europes-borders-open-sweden-denmark-id-2529560-Jan2016/ (accessed Oct. 18th, 2016).

Alves, Rubem (1969): *A Theology of Human Hope*, Washington D. C.: Corpus Books.

Anselm, Reiner (2015): Politische Ethik, in: Wolfgang Huber, Torsten Meireis, Hans-Richard Reuter (eds.), *Handbuch Evangelische Ethik*, München: C. H. Beck, 195–263.

Bonhoeffer, Dietrich (1934): Die Kirche vor der Judenfrage, in: *DBW* XII (1997), 349–358 (originally published 1934).

Brotschi, Markus (2016): SVP-Initiative kann Menschenrechte nicht aushebeln, *Tagesanzeiger* 08/10/2016, http://www.tagesanzeiger.ch/schweiz/standard/svpinitiative-kann-menschenrechte-nicht-aushebeln/story/28468796 (accessed Oct. 18th, 2016).

Burke, Daniel (2016): The guilt-free gospel of Donald Trump, *CNN.com* 10/24/2016, http://edition.cnn.com/2016/10/21/politics/trump-religion-gospel/ (accessed Feb. 23rd, 2017).

Barber, Benjamin A. (1984): *Strong Democracy. Participatory Politics for a New Age*, Oakland: University of California Press.

Barth, Karl (1946): Christengemeinde und Bürgergemeinde, in: Karl Barth, *Rechtfertigung und Recht. Christengemeinde und Bürgergemeinde. Evangelium und Gesetz*, Zürich 1978: TVZ (originally published 1946).

Crouch, Colin (2004): *Post-Democracy*, Oxford: Oxford University Press.

EKD (Evangelische Kirche in Deutschland) (2007): *Gott in der Stadt. Perspektiven evangelischer Kirche in der Stadt*, EKD-Texte 93, Hannover.

EKD (2014): *Engagement und Indifferenz. Kirchenmitgliedschaft als soziale Praxis.* V. EKD-Erhebung über Kirchenmitgliedschaft, Hannover.

Habermas, Jürgen (1992), *Faktizität und Geltung. Beiträge zur Diskurstheorie des Rechts und des demokratischen Rechtsstaats*, Frankfurt am Main: Suhrkamp.

Haddad, Emmanuel (2017): Au Liban, Marine Le Pen tente de rallier les chrétiens, *La Croix* 02/21/2017, http://www.la-croix.com/Religion/Laicite/Au-Liban-Marine-Le-Pen-tente-rallier-chretiens-2017-02-21-1200826473 (accessed Feb. 22nd, 2017).

Hähnig, Anne (2016): Oh Gott, Sachsen!, *Die Zeit* 03/11/2016, http://www.zeit.de/2016/11/kirche-sachsen-fluechtlinge-pegida-homosexualitaet-hilfe/ (accessed Feb. 23rd, 2017).

Haller, Günther (2015): "Lügenpresse!" Ein neuer alter Kampfruf, *DiePresse.com* 01/03/2015, http://diepresse.com/home/zeitgeschichte/4628933/Luegenpresse-Ein-neuer-alter-Kampfruf (accessed Sept. 20th, 2016).

Heitmeyer, Wilhelm (2007): Was hält die Gesellschaft zusammen? Problematische Antworten auf soziale Desintegration, in: Wilhelm Heitmeyer (ed.) (2007), *Deutsche Zustände*, Vol. 5, Frankfurt am Main: Suhrkamp, 37–47.

Höhne, Florian, van Oorschot, Friederike (eds.) (2015): *Grundtexte öffentlicher Theologie*, Leipzig: EVA.

Honecker, Martin (1990): *Einführung in die Theologische Ethik. Grundlagen und Grundbegriffe*, Berlin, New York: de Gruyter.

Hüpping, Sandra, Reinecke, Jost (2007): Abwärtsdriftende Regionen. Die Bedeutung sozioökonomischer Entwicklungen für Orientierungslosigkeit und Gruppenbezogene Menschenfeindlichkeit, in: Wilhelm Heitmeyer (ed.) (2007), *Deutsche Zustände*, Vol. 5, Frankfurt am Main: Suhrkamp, 77–101.

IDEA (2107a): Voter Turnout in Europe, *International Institute for Democracy and Electoral Assistance (IDEA)*, http://www.idea.int/data-tools/continent-view/Europe/40 (accessed Feb. 27th, 2017).

IDEA (2017b): Voter Turnout in the USA, *International Institute for Democracy and Electoral Assistance (IDEA)*, http://www.idea.int/data-tools/country-view/295/40 (accessed Feb. 27th, 2017).

IDEA (2017c): Voter Turnout in South Africa, *International Institute for Democracy and Electoral Assistance (IDEA)*, http://www.idea.int/data-tools/country-view/310/40 (accessed Feb. 27th, 2017).

Jacobs, Ben (2017): Trump attacks 'dishonest media' while making false claims at Florida rally, *The Guardian* 02/19/2017, https://www.theguardian.com/us-news/2017/feb/18/donald-trump-attacks-press-dishonest-media-florida-rally (accessed Feb. 28th, 2017).

Lefort, Claude (1990): Die Frage der Demokratie, in: Ulrich Rödel (ed.), *Autonome Gesellschaft und libertäre Demokratie*, Frankfurt am Main: Suhrkamp, 281–297.

Luther, Martin (1523), Von weltlicher Obrigkeit, wie weit man ihr Gehorsam schuldig sei, in: Martin Luther, WA 11, 245–281.

Maheshwari, Sapna (2017): 10 Times Trump Spread Fake News, *The New York Times* 01/18/2017, https://www.nytimes.com/interactive/2017/business/media/trump-fake-news.html?_r=0 (accessed Feb. 28th, 2017).

Meireis, Torsten (2005): "Sie waren ein Herz und eine Seele und hatten alles gemeinsam" oder "Wer nicht arbeiten will, soll auch nicht essen"? Protestantische Motive im Kontext von Wohlfahrtsstaatlichkeit, in: Karl Gabriel (ed.), *Europäische Wohlfahrtsstaatlichkeit. Soziokulturelle Grundlagen und religiöse Wurzeln*, Jahrbuch für Christliche Sozialwissenschaften, 46, 15–43.

Meireis, Torsten (2008): *Tätigkeit und Erfüllung. Protestantische Ethik im Umbruch der Arbeitsgesellschaft*, Tübingen: Mohr Siebeck.

Meireis, Torsten (2013a): Politischer Gottesdienst als öffentliche Theologie – Bedeutung, Rahmen und theologische Bedingungen, in: Kathrin Kusmierz, David Plüss (eds.), *Politischer Gottesdienst!?*, Zürich: TVZ, 153–175.

Meireis, Torsten (2013b): Die theokratische Frage. Zur politischen Ethik des Heidelberger Katechismus, in: Martin Hirzel, Frank Mathwig, Matthias Zeindler (eds.), *Der Heidelberger Katechismus. Ein reformierter Schlüsseltext*, Zürich: TVZ, 189–218.

Moltmann, Jürgen (1970): Politische Theologie, in: Jürgen Moltmann, *Umkehr zur Zukunft*, München: Kaiser, 168–187.

Nassehi, Armin (2015): "Die arbeiten nichts." Eine kleine Polemik gegen den "Wirtschaftsflüchtling", *Kursbuch*, 183, 101–111.

Niebuhr, Reinhold (1932): *Moral Man and Immoral Society: A Study of Ethics and Politics,* Louisville, KY 2013: Westminster John Know Press (originally published 1932).

Pabst, Adrian (2016): Is Liberal Democracy Sliding into 'Democratic Despotism'? *The Political Quarterly*, Vol. 87, No. 1, January–March, 91–95.

Pannenberg, Wolfhart (1973): *Wissenschaftstheorie und Theologie*, Frankfurt am Main: Suhrkamp.

Pausch, Eberhard (2013): Demokratie innerhalb der Kirche? Zehn Thesen, *Deutsches Pfarrerblatt*, 9/2013, http://www.pfarrerverband.de/pfarrerblatt/index.php?a=show&id=3448 (accessed March 1st, 2013).

Prömpers, Klaus (2017): Wie steht Trump zur Religion? "Er versucht, das ganze Spektrum abzudecken", *domradio.de* 01/19/2017, https://www.domradio.de/themen/weltkirche/2017-01-19/wie-steht-trump-zur-religion (accessed Feb. 22nd, 2017).

Reinhard, Doreen (2016): Kein Erbarmen. Ein Pfarrer outet sich in Internetforen als AfD-nah. Jetzt ist er arbeitslos. Hat er das verdient? *Die Zeit* 08/12/2016, http://www.zeit.de/2016/51/evangelische-kirche-pfarrer-afd-entlassung/komplettansicht (accessed Jan. 31st, 2017).

Richter, Christoph (2017): Kirche und Politik. Der Pfarrer a. D. und die AfD, *Deutschlandfunk* 01/16/2017, http://www.deutschlandfunk.de/kirche-und-politik-der-pfarrer-a-d-und-die-afd.886.de.html?dram:article_id=376330 (accessed Feb. 22nd, 2017)

Ritterband, Charles E. (2012): Konzession wider Willen gegen aussen – neue antidemokratische Massnahme im Innern. Orban beugt sich der "Macht der Europäischen Union", *Neue Zürcher Zeitung* 01/21/2012, http://www.nzz.ch/orban-beugt-sich-der-macht-der-europaeischen-union-1.14441097 (accessed Oct. 18th, 2016).

Salzborn, Samuel (2015): Schleichende Transformation zur Diktatur. Ungarns Abschied von der Demokratie, *Kritische Justiz*, Vol. 48, No. 1, 71–82.

Schumpeter, Joseph A. (2003): *Capitalism, Socialism and Democracy*, London, New York: Routledge (originally published 1943).

Smith, Gregory A., Martínez, Jessica (2016): How the faithful voted: A preliminary 2016 analysis, *PewResearchCenter* 11/09/2016, http://www.pewresearch.org/fact-tank/2016/11/09/how-the-faithful-voted-a-preliminary-2016-analysis/ (accessed Jan. 31st, 2017).

Sölle, Dorothee (1971): *Politische Theologie. Auseinandersetzung mit Rudolf Bultmann*, Stuttgart: Kreuz.

Statista (2016a): Wahlbeteiligung bei den Europawahlen von 1979–2014, *statistic*_id12230_wahlbeteiligung-bei-den-europawahlen-bis-2014.png (accessed Jun. 22nd 2016).

Statista (2016b): Wahlbeteiligung bei den Bundestagswahlen in Deutschland von 1949–2013, *statistic*_id2274_wahlbeteiligung-bei-bundestagswahlen-in-deutschland-seit-1949.png (accessed Jun. 22nd 2016).

Staufenberg, Jess (2016): Boris Johnson 'lied to the British people' and must be a credible Foreign Secretary, says French counterpart, *Independent* 07/14/2016, http://www.independent.co.uk/news/uk/politics/boris-johnson-foreign-secretary-france-french-liar-brexit-eu-government-a7136366.html (accessed March 1st, 2017).

Sundberg, Jan (2015): Who are the nationalist Finns Party? *BBC* 05/11/2015, http://www.bbc.com/news/world-europe-32627013 (accessed March 1st, 2017).

Tanner, Mathias, Müller, Felix, Mathwig, Frank, Lienemann, Wolfgang (eds.) (2009): *Streit um das Minarett. Zusammenleben in der religiös pluralistischen Gesellschaft*, Zürich: TVZ.

The Local (2016): How Swedes would vote if an election were held today, *The Local* 12/01/2016, http://www.thelocal.se/20161201/heres-how-swedes-would-vote-if-an-election-were-held-today (accessed March 1st, 2017).

Tillich, Paul (1932): *Die sozialistische Entscheidung,* Berlin: Medusa 1980 (originally published 1932).

Troeltsch, Ernst (1904), *Politische Ethik und Christentum*, Göttingen: Vandenhoeck.

Troeltsch, Ernst (1912), *Die Soziallehren der christlichen Kirchen und Gruppen*, Tübingen: Mohr.

Tutu, Desmond (1982): *Crying in the Wilderness. The Struggle for Justice in South Africa*, Grand Rapids: Eerdmans.

Valeurs actuelles (2017): Chrétien et gaulliste: Marine Le Pen juge Fillon "opportuniste", *Valeurs actuelles.com* 02/10/2017, http://www.valeursactuelles.com/politique/chretien-et-gaulliste-marine-le-pen-juge-fillon-opportuniste-59598 (accessed Feb. 22nd, 2017).

Verseck, Keno (2015): Gelenkte Demokratie. Wie Viktor Orbán Ungarn putinisiert, *Cicero* 02/20/2015, http://cicero.de/ungarn-im-spannungsfeld-zwischen-eu-und-russland-wie-viktor-orban-ungarn-putinisiert/58894 (acessed Oct. 18th, 2016).

Wernicke, Christian (2015): Wahlerfolg für Front National, *Süddeutsche Zeitung* 12/06/2015, http://www.sueddeutsche.de/politik/frankreich-wahlerfolg-fuer-front-national-1.2771051 (accessed Oct. 18th, 2016).

Winterbauer, Jörg (2016): EU Kommissionspapier: "Polen hält sich nicht an demokratische Standards", *WeltN24* 05/23/2016, https://www.welt.de/politik/ausland/article155597713/Polen-haelt-sich-nicht-an-demokratische-Standards.html (accessed Oct. 18th, 2016).

Wirtschaftswoche (2016): "Freiheit, Gleichheit, Demokratie!" Demonstrationen in Polen, *Wirtschaftswoche* 06/05/2016, http://www.wiwo.de/politik/europa/freiheit-gleichheit-demokratie-demonstrationen-in-polen/13689740.html (accessed Oct. 18th, 2016)

Blasphemy – a Civil-Religious Crime

Rolf Schieder

Blasphemy is the opposite of euphemization and eulogy. Believers are expected to praise and worship God. But history has shown us situations in which God is reviled and derided. Blasphemy is the defamation of God. The motives are diverse: disappointment, rage, and despair, or the wish to shake up and provoke fellow believers, or else to express a new experience of God by negating other experiences of God: "There is no God – except God!" In one of his last songs, Leonhard Cohen calls God an uncompassionate, power-hungry player who does not seem to be the light of the world, but rather one who loves darkness: "You want it darker!" is a blasphemous provocation.

> If you are the dealer, I'm out of the game
> If you are the healer, it means I'm broken and lame
> If thine is the glory then mine must be the shame
> You want it darker
> We kill the flame
>
> Magnified, sanctified, be thy holy name
> Vilified, crucified, in the human frame
> A million candles burning for the help that never came
> You want it darker
>
> Hineni, hineni
> I'm ready, my lord
>
> […]
>
> They're lining up the prisoners
> And the guards are taking aim
> I struggled with some demons
> They were middle class and tame
> I didn't know I had permission to murder and to maim
> You want it darker
>
> Hineni, hineni
> I'm ready, my lord
>
> […]

Cohen's blasphemy is neither cheap nor superficial. It has its foundation in decades of reading the Bible, in existential dealings with the Jewish legacy. Twelve times he quotes Abraham's answer to God's call in Genesis 22:1 – the beginning of the story that Christians call the "sacrifice of Isaac" and Jews the "Akeda", the binding of Isaac. One way or the other, it is a dark story in which God – depending on the interpretation – demands obedience and a human sacrifice or prevents the latter just in time. Leonard Cohen, at any rate, assumes the worst – and so his "I'm ready, my Lord!" is actually mockery. He would like to be "out of the game" – if only he could be. His blasphemy is a desperate protest.

1. Blasphemy in theological perspective: blasphemy is religiously productive

From a theological perspective, blasphemy is a communication event between a believer and his God. Many believers praise and extol their God, ask Him for help, and lament their sufferings to Him. They ask, "Where art thou?", but also "Why hast thou forsaken me?" Only seldom do they revile Him. But situations are imaginable in which a believer despairs of God and wants to provoke Him with an insult. Blasphemy is an event within a relationship – initially between a believer and his God and, to the degree that the reviling is made publicly, between the one reviling God and his fellow believers. These have to live with the loss of consensus and endure the dissent. This demands tolerance from both sides, because what some consider blasphemy is a new truth for others.

Since atheists and agnostics do not believe in any god, and since, from a theological perspective, blasphemy presupposes a relationship to God, contemptuous remarks from atheists about some God alien to them cannot be regarded as blasphemy. They can be considered like contemptuous remarks about an unfamiliar food. The ignorance devalues itself. Outrage on the part of believers, who may be convinced that they have to protect their God, is inappropriate. God Himself knows best how to deal with blasphemy. At any rate, believers, not to mention the state, are unsuitable guardians of His honor. God may defend Himself.

Especially for Christians, blasphemy has a religiously productive aspect. Jesus Himself was accused of blasphemy. What may initially seem like blasphemy can thus prove to be extremely fruitful theologically. The history of religion is full of examples in which the experience of a new relationship to God led to separations and new foundations. As St. Paul reports in 1.Corinthians, many contemporaries regarded the "Word of the Cross" as an irrational, scandalous blasphemy. And indeed, a crucified God who exposes Himself to people's scorn and ridicule is a provocation.

The God of the Christians humiliates Himself, damages His own reputation forever. He makes Himself the object of public derision and as such He is the living God. He is less worried about His own honor than about that of human beings.

In the Age of the Reformation, people were quick to make accusations of blasphemy. Today Voltaire's observation that what is seen as blasphemy in Paris and Rome is considered orthodox in Berlin and Amsterdam became even more complex, since due to the end of the territorial principle and the rise of the principle of pluralism orthodoxy and blasphemy can be found in Paris, Rome, Berlin and Amsterdam at the same time. Under the conditions of principled pluralism, it would be absurd if, for example, Muslims regarded the Jewish and the Christian worship of God as blasphemy. That would make the accusation of blasphemy lasting, and it would end only when all humankind professed the true religion – forced to do so by violence. Instead the human right to error also in religious matters must be remembered. However convinced one may be of the truth of one's own relationship to God, it does not give one the right to force it on others. Peace greatly depends on believers accepting different concepts of God and different religious practices. A plurality of religious practices is no attack on one's own understanding of God or on one's own God. Adherents of another faith can express contempt for my belief. If they thereby insult me, I can charge them in court with insulting my person – not on charges of insulting my God, but my religious feelings. Religious communities can develop theologically through blasphemies. If differences are insurmountable, the community can split and go separate ways. This is a normal process in religious history. But under the conditions of guaranteed individual religious freedom that includes the right to convert, there is no good theological reason for a political intervention.

2. Blasphemy in political perspective

2.1 Religious freedom implies freedom to blasphemy

In 1952, the Supreme Court of the United States passed a historical judgment. In *Joseph Burstyn, Inc. vs. Wilson*, a film distribution company against a New York authority, the explanation of the decisive reasons for the decision in favor of the company reads: "It is not the business of government in our nation to suppress real or imagined attacks upon a particular religious doctrine." And the judges were even clearer in the comprehensive explanation of their judgment: "From the standpoint of freedom of speech and the press, a state has no legitimate interest in protecting any or all religions from views distasteful to them […]"[1]

Although some states in the United States still have blasphemy laws,[2] the Supreme Court's decision of 1952 was still pioneering: in the US, the state believes in the capacity of society to regulate conflicts of worldview without state intervention. This trust has been good for religious discourse. Religious communities and the media feel responsible for a culture of respectful mutual dealings. This became quite clearly visible when leading media like the New York Times, the Washington Post, and CNN refused to reprint the controversial Mohammed caricatures of a Danish newspaper.

Many European intellectuals regarded that as cowardice and a lack of solidarity with the attacked European media. The American media, in contrast, pointed to the different culture of communication in religious matters. In Europe, attacking a religious community can still be interpreted as an act of political liberation and a contribution to societal progress. In the United States, this strategy gains little traction. Since the country's founding, religious institutions have been perceived as partners of freedom, not as its foes. Their social capital is as highly esteemed as their contribution to overcoming racial segregation, integrating migrants, and caring for the poor. In Europe, in contrast, as Alexis des Tocqueville rightly observed, the Churches marched for centuries side by side with the enemies of freedom. Criticism of the Church was simultaneously criticism of the ruling classes. Criticism of religion was thus an act of emancipation. The pathos of emancipation still plays a central role in the criticism of Islam in Europe today.

When we turn the focus to Eastern Europe, it becomes evident that blasphemous criticism of religion aims at a critique of political rule. In 2012, when Pussy Riot performed its "Punk prayer" in the Cathedral of Christ the Savior in Moscow two weeks before the presidential elections, it was clear that the intent was not to deride Orthodox piety, but the political system that suppressed human rights and freedom. The liberal Orthodox theologian Andrey Kurayev suggested to interpret Pussy Riot's performance as a carnivalesque one, as fools' play that – like every carnival – aims to draw attention to abuses. He was not in favor of the Church press-

---

1 https://supreme.justia.com/cases/federal/us/343/495/case.html

2 http://centreforinquiry.ca/blasphemy-laws-still-exist-in-the-united-states/

ing for criminal charges,[3] but the majority of the clergy, the majority of the Russian population, and above all the Putin regime pressed for draconic punishment – despite the activists' assertion that their action had had also a Christian motivation. The Russian state and the Orthodox Church formed a power bloc that proved to be impervious to international protests.

The Pussy Riot affair shows that agitation about blasphemy is especially high when it goes hand in hand with *lese majesty*. In those regions of the world where no consciousness of the necessary distinction between political and religious power has developed, either blasphemy laws are in effect that violate human rights or the societal climate fosters pogroms. If blasphemy were solely a theological problem, it would be easy to resolve. What makes it so difficult to grasp it conceptually, however, is that it is a global *political* problem.

2.2 The Iranian Revolution as the beginning of a new religio-political era: Western individual autonomy against Islamic collective heteronomy?

With his fatwa against Salman Rushdie Ayatollah Khomeini effectively used the accusation of blasphemy as a global political weapon. This fatwa can be read as the declaration of a global culture war against the West. Khomeini ignored national, constitutional, and international legal limits. The writer's life is in danger at all times in all places. The attempt to charge Salman Rushdie, a British citizen, with blasphemy under British law failed only because the British blasphemy law still valid at that time protected solely the Church of England, but not other religious communities.

While many critics of Islam in Germany may be xenophobic, apocalyptic, and populist, this does not mean to deny the antagonistic conflicts between Islamic and Western culture. In many Islamic countries, blasphemy is punished by death. Each individualized expression of faith is seen as a threat to an imagined collective whole.. According to this political culture, collective heteronomy should not only dominate individual autonomy, it should make the latter even impossible. The threat alone is enough to intimidate and creates a climate of fear.

---

3 On this, cf. Joachim Willems: *Pussy Riots Punk-Gebet. Religion, Recht und Politik in Russland*, Cologne: Berlin University Press 2013, 89f.

This stands in opposition to the basic values of Western societies. The conflict in the West over the Islamic headscarf is symptomatic: those who would like to forbid it and those who defend its wearers actually agree that women's rights to self-determination are to be defended. The best way to ensure this is for the one side to ban the headscarf as a symbol of heteronomy; the other side wants to protect women's autonomy by opposing state interventions. While radical critics of Islam see in the beheading of unbelievers and the veiling of women acts of negating individuality critics of the critics of Islam draw attention to a heteronomous tendency in the actions the critics of Islam: those who want to strengthen Western culture aim at a cultural hegemony. But this is to pursue a self-contradictory political strategy: to ban the headscarf is a heteronomous prescription of supposed symbolic autonomy.

3. Blasphemy as a civil religious practice

3.1 From libeling God to sacralizing the social

Last year, two highly stimulating books on the history of blasphemy in France were published. One was written by Jacques de Saint Victor and bears the prosaic title "Blasphème. Brève histoire d'un 'crime imaginaire'". The book by Anastasia Colosimo has a much more dramatic title: "Les bûchers de la liberté". As different as the authors are in style and choice of material, they are united in their concern that freedom of expression and the principle of *laïcité* are being increasingly eroded in France. The respect for the deep convictions of others has become a contemporary dogma. But quite often the supposed respect is disguised fear. Both authors note that the convictions of Montesquieu or Voltaire today are considered atheistic by some, racist and Islamophobic by others.[4] Instead of defending the beliefs of the individual, now the means of the state are being used to defend the convictions of whole groups. But precisely this con-

4 Ibid., 119: "La pensée de Montesquieu, de Beccaria, de Voltaire y est aujourd'hui tenue pour 'sectaire' et 'athée' par les uns, pour 'islamophobe' et 'rasciste' par les autres."

tradicts the basic principle of *laïcité*, which always protects the believer, but never any religion.[5]

Anastasia Colosimo argues similarly to Saint Victor, though much more passionately. She felt that the attacks on *Charlie Hebdo* called on her to defend not only freedom of expression, but also and explicitly the right to irreligiosity and profanation. Precisely for that reason, she was outraged that "the victims of the attack on *Charlie Hebdo*, who, during their lifetimes, described themselves as 'profaners'" after their deaths "were declared sacred, not merely heroized, but canonized, as it were".[6] All their lives, she wrote, the authors had struggled against sanctification and canonization of any kind and they saw the absolute meaning of their profession in lasting desacralization. What a fate: irreligious people, who wanted to liberate society from religion, were stylized as civil-religious icons post mortem. Incidentally, the German colleagues from the satire magazine *Titanic* also clearly saw that something about the collective memorialization of *Charlie Hebdo* wasn't right. While almost every politician and public intellectual wore a "Je suis Charlie" button, the Titanic staff published a photo of itself on which each of them introduced himself with his name: "Je suis Holger", "Je suis Lena", etc. One person in the last row, though, showed a sign reading: "Je t'aime".

With the aid of the court judgments and legislative procedures of the last twenty years, Colosimo reconstructs the increasing civil-religious charging of societal discourse. She regards the European Court of Human Rights' 1994 ruling in the case *Otto-Preminger-Institut vs. Österreich* as groundbreaking. The country of Austria had prohibited the institute from showing the controversial film "Council of Love", which shows a love scene between Jesus and Virgin Mary. Austria feared unrest among the Catholic populace of Tyrol. The European Court then had to decide whether this ban violated § 10 of the European Convention on Human Rights. The majority of the judges rejected this with the explanation that expressions of hurtful and insulting opinions could be tolerated only if these contributed to a public debate that was capable of promoting "progress in human affairs". From now on, every provocative expression of an

5 Ibid., 118: "La laïcité a toujours protégé les croyants mais n'a jamais protégé aucune religion."

6 Colosimo 2016, 31: "[L]es victimes de l'attentat contre *Charlie Hebdo* qui se décrivaient volontiers de leur vivant comme des profanateurs ont été sacralisées après leur mort, non seulement héroisées mais aussi en quelque façon sanctifiées."

opinion could be subjected to this test of "progress", whereby translating the formulation "progress in human affairs" is not simple. In French, we read that hurtful expressions must contribute to some "forme de débat public capable de favoriser le progrès dans les affaires du genre humain". A German translation like "Fortschritt in menschlichen Angelegenheiten" places too little emphasis on the political character of "human affairs". Ultimately, the point is gaining progress in understanding human dignity and human rights. But of course, what such a "progress in humanity" is can be judged only *ex post*. The criterion invoked by the Court is thus greatly in need of interpretation. The negative distinction is more plausible: a constructive and productive meaning should inhere in a provocation. An insult whose only goal is to insult ("gratuitously offensive") is condemned.

The understanding of blasphemy has changed over the decades. Colosimo states: "The victim is no longer the Divinity, but the community whose god has been insulted. But this deifies the community."[7] European blasphemy legislation, she says, displays the tendency "to sacralize societal cohesion and public peace, in other words civility".[8] So, whoever wants to study the increase of civil religion in Western democracies need only pursue the change in blasphemy laws. This also applies to the 1969 German reform of the blasphemy laws: neither God nor the communities of believers are from now on protected, but public peace. Blasphemy laws are laws on civil religion: they protect the prevailing civil-religious consensus and serve the imagined cohesion of the community.[9]

The civil-religious significance of blasphemy laws became obvious already in early modern times: sacrality was transferred from the Church to the State. The dictionary of the Académie Française includes the term "blasphèmes contre la patrie". Blasphemy increasingly means lack of reverence for something to which reverence is due, the desacralization of something regarded as sacred, a provocation that seeks to profane. But what is to be considered sacred varies from nation to nation. What is considered blasphemy in Rome, Paris, and Madrid – as Voltaire observed – is orthodox in Berlin, Copenhagen, and London. Instead of a confessional context for blasphemy, now the political sphere itself becomes religiously

---

7 Ibid., 109: "La victime n'est plus la Divinité, mais la communauté dont la Divinité a été offensée, et par là, la communauté divinisée."

8 Ibid., 109: the tendency: "sacraliser la cohésion et la paix publique, autrement dit la civilité".

9 Ibid., 108: the problem: "la démocratie qui nécessiterait elle-même d'être sacralisée".

charged. Accordingly, the French blasphemy law of 17 May 1819 reads: "Tout outrage à la morale publique et religieuse, ou aux bonnes moeurs [...] sera puni d'un emprisonnement d'un mois à un an [...]."[10] Religion, morals, and common decency form a civil-religious unity. Schleiermacher's protest against the mixing of bourgeois morality and religion would have found listeners in France, as well. In 1881 a law completely guaranteeing freedom of opinion and the press was passed. France was thus the first country in Europe that no longer made blasphemy punishable.

3.2 Victimhood and memory laws: metamorphoses of blasphemy

Between 1972 and 2015, however, a whole series of laws were passed in France that limited freedom of expression. Referring to the UN International Convention on the Elimination of All Forms of Racial Discrimination of 1965, in 1972 "offenses à caractère raciste" were made punishable. This was supplemented in 1990; from now on, to deny the existence of "crimes contre l'humanité" was punishable. France was thereby the first country to adopt a "loi mémorielle". It sought to punish those who denied the Shoah. In 2004, a momentous supplement was added: ""Those who... have caused discrimination, hatred, or violence against a person or a group of persons because of their origin or their membership or non-belonging to a particular ethnic group, nation, race, or religion shall be punished with imprisonment for one month to one year..."[11] This added insulting an ethnic group, a nation, or a religion to insulting a race. There is no longer a distinction between racist insulting and insulting a religious community. In her detailed study "The Right to Religious Freedom in International Law. Between Group Rights and Individual Rights", Anat Scolnicov notes: "Legislation against religious hate speech should follow an approach that distinguishes between permissible offensive speech against ideas and impermissible offensive speech against people *qua* members of a religious group." (2011, 209)

---

10 Ibid., 146.

11 "Ceux qui, [...], auront provoqué à la discrimination, à la haine ou à la violence à l'égard d'une personne ou d'un groupe de personnes à raison de leur origine ou de leur appartenance ou de leur non-appartenance à une éthnie, une nation, une race oủ une religion determinée, seront punis d'un emprisonnement d'un mois à un an [...]", quoted after Colosimo 2016, 155.

In France since 2004, religious communities that feel insulted can charge journalists, authors, and publishers with a crime and thereby undermine freedom of the press and expression – and all on the ostensibly virtuous basis of protecting victims. But what if the ostensible victims paint themselves as such simply in order to secure advantages for themselves? In their 2009 study "The Empire of Trauma. An Inquiry into the Condition of Victimhood", Didier Fassin and Richard Rechtmann impressively described the transformation of the discourse on victimhood in Western societies. The moral economy of these societies has shifted, they maintain. Whoever is in a position to stylize himself as a victim can greatly improve his standing. Admired is no longer the heroic, but the tragic. So, when "victims" are publicly identified, one must examine very closely whether the issue is indeed appropriate protection for victims, or whether the concept of the victim is being used to improve one's position in the political discourse. The victimization discourse provides a huge reservoir of potential outrage. Those who make the accusation of blasphemy can present themselves as "victims of a blasphemy". This offers them many strategic advantages, while those who regard the critique of religion as a political act of liberation and a call for freedom of expression have difficulties to get a hearing in public discourse.

In France between 1984 and 2009, there were twenty trials on charges of insulting a religious community. Eighteen of them were initiated by Catholic groups and two by Muslims. In 2001, the writer Michel Houellebecq was charged in response to his statement that Islam was "la religion la plus con", but he was acquitted because he had expressed disdain solely for Islam, not for any specific believer. On 22 March 2007, *Charlie Hebdo*, too, was acquitted of charges of insulting Muslims. In its explanation, the court pointed out that freedom of expression could indeed be limited if someone merely wanted to insult someone else without making a contribution to the "progrès dans les affaires du genre humain" – a quotation from the ECtHR ruling from 1984. Both suits pressed by Muslims were dismissed, Catholic groups succeeded in two cases.

The fundamental problem in France seems to be that the increasingly detailed limitations of freedom of expression undermine the secularity of the state. Colosimo notes: "The metamorphosis of the blasphemy offense into a racist offense is a clear sign."[12] Religious groups can force the state

---

12 "La metamorphose du délit de blaspheme en délit raciste en est un signe éminent." 199.

to make legal rulings in religious matters by invoking the protection of minorities, the prohibition of discrimination, and protection against racism. This also applies to the legislation protecting the memory of the Shoah, because the law on the Shoah leads many groups of victims to urge that their "holy" history as victims become part of the state's culture of memory as well. In 2005, the initiative "Liberté pour l'Histoire" published an appeal signed by more than 1,000 historians that contains the passage: "History is not a religion. The historian accepts no dogma, respects no ban, knows no taboos."[13] If the state raises a historical event to the status of a dogma, then this is a veritable civil-religious act. In Germany, too, the memory of the Shoah has a civil-religious status. The scandal over Martin Walser's protest against the instrumentalization of the Shoah for civil-religious purposes shows the degree to which his speech in the Paulskirche was felt to be blasphemous.

On 13 November 2014, a law was promulgated in France that made "justifying terrorism" a crime. In 2015, there were already seventy trials pending under this law. A tendency to increasingly limit freedom of expression is unmistakable. This is also true of the ECtHR's rulings, incidentally. On 13 September 2005, it commented on Turkey's blasphemy laws, noting that freedom of expression is always tied to certain responsibilities. And it continued: "Among them, in the context of religious beliefs, may legitimately be included a duty to avoid expressions that are gratuitously offensive to others and profane. [...] This being so, as a matter of principle it may be considered necessary to punish improper attacks on objects of religious veneration."

4. Blasphemy in German criminal law: from civil-religious instrumentalization to the protection of freedom of expression

In his essay "Der strafrechtliche Schutz der Religion in Deutschland. Geschichte, aktuelle Herausforderungen und kriminalpolitische Überlegungen" (2016), Martin Heger notes that, for the confessionally bound state of early modern times, protecting "its" religion was also the core of its statehood. The territorial state integrated itself through a unified religion. "He who blasphemed against the God of the respective ruler at the same time

13 http://www.lph-asso.fr/index.php?option=com_content&view =article&id=2&Itemid=13&lang=en

insulted the majesty of the sovereign, thereby questioning the foundation of the sacredly based power as such." (Heger 2016, 110)

From 1871 to 1969, Germany had a law against blasphemy whose wording did not change: "Whoever creates a nuisance by publicly blaspheming against God in abusive expressions or who publicly reviles one of the Christian Churches or another religious community existing in the state under public law or its institutions and customs, or similarly whoever conducts reviling mischief in a church or in another place intended for religious gatherings, shall be punished with imprisonment for up to three years." (§ 166 StGB) Jewish congregations often sought the protection of § 166 StGB. The paragraph no longer presupposed a religiously homogenous territory. Its aim was solely the protection of the religious communities. § 166 StGB thus stands in the same line as the threat of punishment for crimes against honor (StGB185 ff.) and hate speech (130 StGB).

In 1969, § 166 StGB was changed in two ways. From now on, so called "Weltanschauungsgemeinschaften" enjoy the same protection under penal law as religious communities do. The paragraph was now supplemented with the limiting "suitability to disturb the peace" clause. No longer is every blasphemous speech punishable, but only such speech as is likely to disturb public peace. Heger notes laconically: "Since the change of 1969, § 166 StGB protects the public peace. Neither the individual religious community nor religious peace as a part of public peace is protected – nor individual religious freedom and not solely a value system that favors tolerance or acceptance of other confessions." (Ibid., 122)

In its "Wunsiedel Ruling" of 4 November 2009, Germany's Federal Constitutional Court determined with desirable clarity how high the hurdle must be to find that the public peace is endangered. That some citizens are disturbed is not yet a threat to the public peace. "A disturbance associated with the intellectual debate in the struggle among opinions is the necessary other side of freedom of expression and cannot be a legitimate reason for its limitation. The possible confrontation with disturbing opinions, even if their logical consequence is dangerous and even if they aim at a fundamental revolution of the existing order, is part of a free state." The Court also rejected a limitation of freedom of expression based on pedagogical reasons: "Even the goal of solidifying human rights in the populace's sense of right and wrong does not permit the suppression of opinions contrary to this." So, if someone wants to invoke the endangering of the public peace in order to limit freedom of expression, he must demonstrate that danger precisely: "The goal here is protection against utterances whose content recognizably aims at actions that endanger legal rights, that is, that mark the transition to aggression or violation of the law. The preservation of the public peace thus refers to the external effects of expressions of opinion, for example through appeals or emotionalizations, that trigger in the addressees a willingness to act or that reduce inhibitions or that directly intimidate third parties."[14]

In September 2014, the penal law section of the 70th German Jurists' Conference was presented with a motion to call for the rescinding of § 166 StGB. The following motion was rejected by a broad majority (21/59/8): "The legal category of the offense of reviling a confession (§ 166 StGB) cannot be justified either with the protection of the general public nor with the protection of individual rights and should therefore be rescinded. Speaking in favor of this is also the slight practical significance of this offense." Instead, the Conference accepted the following motion with a majority (62/15/9): "The legal category of the offense of reviling a confession (§ 166 StGB) should be retained, because, in a culturally and religiously increasingly pluralistic society, it, like other freedom-protecting definitions of offenses, performs an admittedly primarily symbolic, but nevertheless legal-politically significant, value-shaping function. It gives religious minorities the feeling of existential security."[15] The civil-religious interest of the German penal jurists is evident – and problematic, because criminal law possesses no mandate to inculcate democracy. Its task is not to educate the nation. But in Germany, the supplementations to the laws against inciting ethnic hatred that make denying the Shoah punishable blur the boundaries between civil-religious control over the populace and its freedom of conscience and expression – quite like in France.

Martin Heger suggests an understanding of § 166 StGB as a *lex specialis* of § 185 StGB, rather than giving it a civil-religious foundation. He also suggests to interpret its criteria narrowly. "Thus, an endangering of the peace is to be examined indeed and not simply presumed; and a vituperation, like abusive criticism, should be assumed only if the defamation of a confession or religious community stands at the center of the expression." (Heger 2016, 140) As an institution, a publicly acting Church ought to be able to endure insults that lie below this threshold. But § 166 StGB should not be entirely eschewed, because in the future, smaller religious communities in particular could very well require an explicit protection. The ele-

---

14 BVerfGE 124, here quoted after Heger (2016), 123.

15 http://www.djt.de/fileadmin/downloads/70/djt_70_Beschluesse_141202.pdf, 11.

gance of Martin Heger's suggestion is that § 166 StGB need not be seen as an anachronistic privileging of religious communities, but precisely as a limitation of possible desires to feel outraged on the part of religious communities. Just as politicians and public figures sometimes have to endure vehement criticism, so, too, religious communities must be able to live with competing opinions and worldviews.

5. Conclusion: who benefits from and who is protected by blasphemy laws?

The blasphemy problem is not a theological, but essentially a civil-religious and religio-political one. The accusation of blasphemy becomes virulent – not only in early modern times, but also today – if a polity sees its civil-religious and moral economy endangered. The increasing sacralization of culture has brought forth metamorphoses of blasphemy that are exacerbated by a mushrooming victimization discourse. Blasphemy laws do not protect God, but the "public peace", in other words: the overall societal consensus.

A theological approach to the problem of blasphemy will thus have to concentrate on a critique of the civil-religious charging of culture. From a Christian perspective, two considerations could act as guidelines: believers should leave it up to God how He wants to respond to blasphemous utterances. He does not need a state penal code. The Christian God, in Jesus Christ on the Cross, made Himself the object of public ridicule, so it can be assumed that He is not interested in subservient obeisance. Rather, we can assume that by becoming a human being, He seeks to point out that we encounter in every person a child of God who deserves respect. This would mean that every insult or injury to another person is ultimately a blasphemous act – precisely from a theological perspective. Protection from blasphemy would then apply no longer to God, nor specifically to His believers, and not to the public peace, but to every individual person as a creature of God.

References

Asad, Talal; Brown, Wendy; Butler, Judith; Mahmood, Saba (2013): *Is Critique Secular? Blasphemy, Injury, and Free Speech*, New York: Fordham University Press.

Colosimo, Anastasia (2016): *Les bûchers de la liberté*, Paris: Éditions Stock.

Heger, Martin (2016): Der strafrechtliche Schutz der Religion in Deutschland - Geschichte, aktuelle Herausforderungen und kriminalpolitische Überlegungen, *Zeitschrift für evangelisches Kirchenrecht* 61, 109–140.

Nash, David (2007): *Blasphemy in the Christian World. A History*, Oxford: Oxford University Press.

Saint Victor, Jacques de (2016): *Blasphème. Brève histoire d'un "crime imaginaire"*, Paris: Gallimard.

Scolnicov, Anat (2011): *The Right to Religious Freedom in International Law. Between Group Rights and Individual Rights*, London: Routledge.

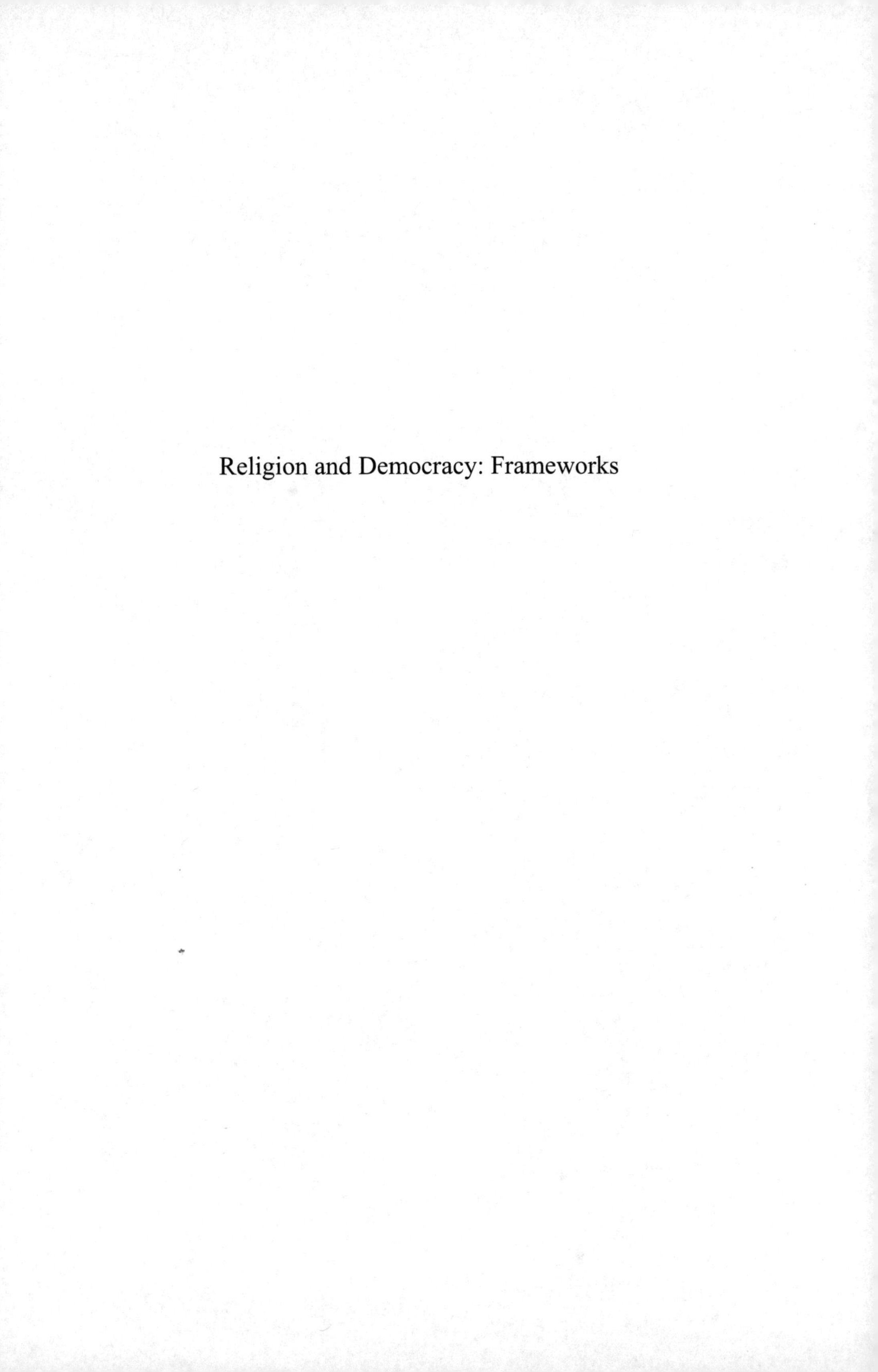

Religion and Democracy: Frameworks

Social Formations of Religion and Their Relevance for Public Theology Worldwide

Andreas Feldtkeller

Introductory remarks

The academic discipline of Comparative Religion is not supposed to engage directly in statements of public theology. Nevertheless, it can contribute to its principles by connecting the purpose of public theology to general observations on social formations of religion and on their role in society. Such observations may help to better analyze the complex relationship between religion and democracy.

In both academia and the media, a multitude of contributions on the role of religion in the political realm opt for "religion" as such – independent of place, time and circumstances – playing a specific role which is depicted as either being harmful because of its backing for the abuse of power or helpful because it supports civic values (Haynes 2010). Another similar set of theses contradicting each other can be found concerning the wide topic of "religion and violence" (Hempelmann 2006).

Most of the papers in question have one thing in common: a lack of analysis concerning the social formation of what they call "religion". They either look at religion as something regulated by scripture and doctrine, unaware of the powerful social factors at play within religion, or they assume that only one, invariant social embodiment of religion exists and that therefore, by the mere use of the notion "religion", they have already made clear what social implications they are talking about. For some, the invariant social expression of religion is a powerful institution; for others it is a league of backward-minded people denying modernity; for again others it is a network of courageous advocates for humanity.

Sociology of religion, being the academic discipline in charge of the relation between religion(s) and social formation, has contributed a lot to our ability to diversify the concept of a social body for religion (Riesebrodt & Konieczny 2010). But still, throughout the history of this discipline, a tendency can be observed to search for the *one* formative principle that is expressed in religion.

During the early period of the discipline, Émile Durkheim, for example, was convinced that the social formation of any religion is determined by how human history of religion began. For him, the idea of "Totemism", conceived as a worldwide primitive form of religion, is the clue for understanding any later social formation of religion. Still this concept made him aware of religion having an inalienable function in modern societies (Durkheim 1912). About the same time, Max Weber derived his model about the social formation of religion from what he observed in European Protestantism. Therefore, he sees the "church" as some sort of norm for the social formation of religion, and in a distinction first published 1906 he understands that any "church" has begun by being something different than a church: a "sect". It has become a "church" only by losing its charismatic form of leadership and by establishing a more stable form of institution based on the authority of official representatives (Weber 1920, 211).

Two generations later, Pierre Bourdieu somehow combined Max Weber's approach of looking at contemporary religion in modern societies and Émile Durkheim's approach starting from what he considered "archaic" religion. As a person having participated in the Algerian war of independence and having added observations from Berber religion to his view of the Catholic Church in France, he built his theory around the dynamics between groups related to priests, prophets and wizards (Bourdieu 1971). Also for Bourdieu, the differentiation of social formations only reaches as far as his observations do, and his theory is not fit to serve as a general explanation throughout the history of religion.

During the last five decades, sociology of religion has extensively been occupied with interpreting and differentiating the concept of "secularization". It has been discussed what specific changes secularization brings about for the role of religion in society. After it had become clear that it was too simplistic to expect the disappearance of religion as such, in general, and everywhere (Joas 2006), almost all the efforts have been put in differentiating the changes that secularization brings about for religion (Martin 2005) – but again it has been widely taken for granted that everybody knows how religion looked like in "traditional" societies before secularization. So far, the hypothesis has not seriously been tested that secularization may only affect specific historically contingent social formations of religion, whereas other social formations of religion that have existed for long time may remain much more stable or even gain from secularization.

In what follows, first a model for a more diversified description of social formations of religion that has previously been published in German (Feldtkeller 2012) will be summarized. The scope of this approach is to combine knowledge from Comparative Religion with observations from Sociology of Religion, thus creating a typology that is apt to cover all the different historical and topographical contexts within human history of religion. In a second step it will be analyzed what potential this model offers to analyze relations between religion and the political realm, and thirdly, based on that, an attempt will be made to describe the role of "public theology" in relation to social formations of religion.

Social formations of religion

(1) The most senior social formations related to religion are *communities of descent* (Müller-Karpe 1998, 65–66). The earliest archeological evidence for religious practices since the Paleolithic Age can be drawn from burials, the circumstances of which indicate that the deceased person maintained importance for the human community performing the burial and preserving the memory of the place (May 1986). There is a close connection between remembering a deceased person and forming a community of descent, because only the memory of ancestors can define a community of descent bigger than the core family of two, three, or four generations living at present (Feldtkeller 2005). All over the world, we find communities that are defined by reference to common ancestors, and normally such reference is performed in rituals and in the repetitive account of mythic narratives. It must be highlighted that communities of descent are in no way "natural" entities; rather they are social constructions, because they depend on cultural markers defining which of the hundreds of possible ancestors are those relevant for the cohesion of the group. Along with the memory of the ancestors, communities of descent are regularly structured by distinctions between age groups (children, youth, parents, elders), gender, and wider or closer family relations. All these distinctions are from time to time reaffirmed and rearranged by rituals.

(2) A second social formation of religion complementing the first one is *relations of cultural exchange*, initially between communities of descent. Within a community of descent, normally all rites and myths are a common good. But also beyond the communities of descent it may happen that parts of the symbolic universe or some elements of it are being exchanged. Occasions for this may be peaceful or hostile encounters between groups,

migration, trade, or exogamic marriages. Already throughout the Paleolithic Age, some cultural traits with religious meaning can be found so geographically widespread that relations of cultural exchange are the most plausible explanation (Ohlig 2002, 34–35). Very early examples for this are specific features of burials, sacrifices, or figures symbolizing human fertility.

(3) With human societies settling down and becoming more complex, the issue of human power over other human beings gained specific relevance for religion. This can be observed from the Neolithic Age, and it is fully unfolded since the earliest imperial societies. Religious symbols become expressions of an *order of power*, legitimizing inequality and the use of force. Egyptian pharaohs, Mesopotamian kings and others following their example had themselves depicted as representatives of personal deities (Kemp 1983, 71–76), and they justified their violence executed against enemies or against subdued groups of population as the realization of a divine cosmic order. Their subjects were forced to practice such expressions of religion as were suitable to acknowledge the order of power, but they were excluded from full participation in the symbolic universe of the ruling class or ethnic group. This means that under such circumstances the social structure of religion becomes much more hierarchical than it had been before. Without question, also communities of descent entail a certain inequality in the distribution of power between age groups and sexes, but now to a much greater extent religious meaning serves the purpose of constructing inequality.

(4) At about the same period within the history of mankind, one further social formation begins to inform the expression of religion: *institutions of knowledge*. There are specialists for the transmission of knowledge also to be found in communities of descent, but more complex societies can organize knowledge in such a way that specific groups are exempted from the burden of producing their own livelihood and are instead enabled to practice the accumulation and transmission of knowledge as a full-time profession (cf. Kemp 1983, 81). From the very beginning, knowledge administered by such elites at least partly served for religious purposes (Schneider 2013, 76–77), and the foundation of the order of knowledge was a religious one. Socially, the institutions of knowledge were structured either in personal relations between teachers and their students or as schools with a more complex form of organization. Knowledge could be transmitted orally within a culture of memory or in writing, which required the introduction of the respective skills – in many cultures interpreted as a divine gift along with knowledge.

(5) The first millennium BCE saw additional innovations in the social embodiment of religion. Now from within the milieu of teachers transmitting religion as a form of knowledge, a new kind of experimental approach to the acquisition of religious knowledge emerged. This happened first in India and was occasionally combined with the idea that every human being suffers from certain shortcomings in human existence, which can only be cured by a *transforming practice* found initiated by an enlightened religious teacher. In consequence of the conviction that the remedy was needed by all mankind, measures were taken to teach the respective religious ideas and practices not only to a limited group of students but to reach – as far as possible – all mankind. For the first time in history, the concept of all mankind belonging together was established. The Buddhist monastic order was for a long time the most successful realization of the new religious setup. Abstinence from marriage, possessions, and stable settlement enabled monks to become transmitters of religious practice with high mobility, thus spreading the message throughout an ever-expanding territory (Gombrich 1995). The typical social structure of religious communities informed by the idea of a transforming practice is a symbiosis between highly specialized transmitters of the practice (here: monks) and their ordinary followers implementing parts of the transforming practice in their everyday lives and sustaining the specialists. For becoming a follower of such practices, there are no requirements concerning the belonging to a certain community of descent or a certain entity of political rule. Therefore, for the first time in the history of mankind, social formations were established that were truly transcultural in their character, inviting every human being to a fellowship of transformation irrespective of its origin.

(6) Again, the new social formation of religion was soon complemented by another form correlating to it. The idea to propagate a transforming praxis beyond any limits has the advantage that it does not exclude anybody, but the downside of it is that without any means of exclusion, all sorts of eclecticism and deviation will occur among the ordinary followers. Once more, Buddhism is the earliest example for this (cf. Wynne 2015, 177–185). To outbalance such disadvantages, besides the completely open communities a different type of transcultural community emerged that equally is open to people from any origin but at the same time restricts access by religious means. Typically, rituals of initiation are being employed for this purpose, preceded or combined with formal instruction and examinations. Obviously, rituals of initiation are not a new feature: they also occur in the context of communities of descent to mark the transition between childhood and adolescence, but now they acquire a differ-

ent social function. The result of performing cultural inclusion combined with religious exclusion are rather small local groups of membership, connected with similar such groups at many different places. This social formation of religion may therefore be called *transcultural network.* Christianity in the second and third century CE mainly represented such a formation (cf. Lössl 2010, 121–124), besides religions like the cult of Mithras and Manicheism. Belonging to such a network offers to its members the advantage that they can travel and will be hosted at any station of their route by a group belonging to the same religious network.

Now as the differentiation of six different social formations of religion has been developed, it needs to be clarified how they can be employed as a heuristic instrument to understand the social setup of religious communities in any concrete historical and geographical context.

As we have seen, the six social formations emerged at different times within the history of mankind. This does not mean that the more senior formations would disappear once the more recent ones have come into being. Rather the diversity of possible social formations of religion was amplified during history. Since the first millennium CE, all the six formations reviewed above are available, and each given religious community at a specific place and time may be described in its overall social setup by one of the formations or – even more likely – by several of them. If social formations of religion are combined with each other, their concrete expression will vary and they will adapt to each other. One formation may become dominant and others may alter their appearance accordingly. In the most complex religious communities, all the six social formations can be observed working together in some way or another.

For almost any religious group, communities of descent (formation 1) are somehow the backbone of its social setup. In urban societies, this may often be reduced to core families, but still it is likely, or even mandatory, that children will follow the religious belonging of their parents and that events in the life of the family are facilitated by rites as they are communicated in the tradition of that specific religious community.

To what extent religious communities entail an order of power (formation 3) as part of their social setup is closely connected to the assumptions about power in the respective society and political order. As far as a political system deals with power as something that is based on religious foundations, it will use the presence of at least one religious community to encode it with symbols legitimizing power, and there will always be representatives of religion ready to accept the advantage in status offered to them in exchange for providing greater legitimacy of power.

The concept of a transforming practice that is bound to be offered to all humankind (formation 5) was for a long time limited to very few, although highly diversified religious communities. Only recently in the context of modernity and of easier worldwide communication it has been adapted by a greater number of religious communities, thereby imitating mainly Buddhist, Christian, or Muslim examples of propagating their teachings in a global horizon.

The changes brought about to religion by recent developments summarized under the notion of "secularization" can be described without introducing new social formations of religion that would not have been known before. What exactly is meant by "secularization" varies from context to context. Typically, secularization entails a reduction or abolition of religious symbols serving the purpose of legitimizing power (formation 3). Along with it, sometimes (but not always) orders of knowledge are disentangled in a way that religious knowledge will be separated from secular knowledge (formation 4). Additionally, secularization may bring about critical hermeneutics that look at religious myths as a symbolic language which needs special interpretation to still be meaningful (formation 1). On the other hand, the importance of cultural exchange in combining religious symbols (formation 2) becomes even greater under conditions of secularization, practices offered as a cure for shortcomings in human nature become more divers (formation 5), and the importance of core families on the one hand (formation 1), transcultural networks on the other hand (formation 6) does in many secular contexts not suffer decline.

Religion and the political realm

Theologians of different religious affiliation are trained to develop their analysis from within the framework of normative scriptures and the respective orthodoxy of their communities (Ritschl 1986). Departing from there, they may overestimate the actual influence of scripture and doctrine on what representatives as well as members of their religious community say and do – and they may underestimate the invisible power of social formations within religion.

Long-term historical records from almost any religious community suggest that the participation in public discourses by religious groups and individuals is not just regulated by scriptures and orthodoxies but also by group interests and relations of power. The social formations of religions as previously described, including their configurations of dominance and subordination, are effective as regulatory principles within the religious communities with at least the same impact as the "official" regulatory principles, scripture, and orthodoxy.

Within many expressions of Christianity, for example, the baptism of small infants has become the established praxis without any strong scriptural reasons that would support a priority of such baptism above the baptism of adolescents or adults as practiced during the time when Christianity still was predominantly a transcultural network. Seen from the perspective of social formation, the baptism of infants ensures that the respective Christian community concerning its strategies for social stabilization behaves like a community of descent (formation 1). It claims all the progeny of its membership for itself, interpreting the interference of any other religious community as an offense. In some contexts, even ethnicity and belonging to a certain Christian denomination are strongly connected to each other – close to the exclusion of persons not belonging to the same ethnic group.

Alike and often associated with this, the role of emperors, kings, or princes in quite a number of Christian communities throughout history since the 4th or 5th century CE has been highlighted in a way that rather resembles Egyptian, Greek, or Roman imperial religion (formation 3) than anything that could be argued from Christian scriptures. Although the New Testament does not offer much argument against the power of monarchic rulers already in office, it does not make provision for the installation of Christian monarchic rulers as they became a dominant political setup within both Eastern and Western Christianity for many centuries.

The model of social formations of religion and their combinations, as presented in the previous paragraph, can be used as a heuristic instrument to better understand the factors at play in the relation between religious communities and the political realm. It helps to understand the limitations of theology in its attempts to structure religious life in harmony with scriptural and doctrinal prerequisites: theology, as we mainly know it, is what becomes of institutions of knowledge (formation 4) in the context of religions informed by the teachings of a transformative praxis (formation 5) or a transcultural network (formation 6). As such, theology will take its place but not without being challenged by the influence of other social formations relevant for the respective religious community.

Arguing against reductionist theories of religion, the model of social formations offers the possibility to disconnect political implications of religion from ontological statements about what religion allegedly is qua being religion. In consequence of the social analysis provided by this model, there is not one single statement about the social or political impact of religion that would be true for every given religion. In other words: religion cannot be defined by one single social or political function. Any claim that there could be universally valid statements about the relation between religion and society suffers from simplification – it rests on an assumption that observations made in one or several specific contexts can be applied to any other historical and geographic context in which religion occurs.

The social factor within religious communities that is closest to being universally valid is the importance of family bonds for the transmission of religious practices from generation to generation. Nevertheless, even to this factor there are quite frequent exemptions: some religious communities take provisions that entry is only acceptable by personal choice, not by heritage. Early Christianity in Mesopotamia took this even further by demanding celibacy from any baptized member, thus preventing transmission from generation to generation (Markschies 1999, 147). In addition, there are so many possibilities of what impact family bonds can have on the relation between religion and the wider context of society that no further almost universal statements can be derived from the observation about the importance of family bonds.

As there are no universally valid statements about the relation between religion and society, there are also no universally invalid statements. If we accept and apply the heuristic instrument of the differentiation in social formations of religion, it is not possible any more to state that no "true" religion will display certain "bad" social or political behaviors and that any community practicing violence can only be considered a distortion of religion. Seen from a descriptive perspective of observation, there is ample evidence for violence, cruelty, justification of inequality, and glorification of power throughout the history of religion. It cannot reasonably be stated that religion is only religion if no such phenomena emanate from it.

Therefore, the scope of possible contributions by religious persons or groups to the political realm is not already limited by the fact that they speak from a religious position. Rather, it all depends on the selection of social formations that are relevant within the specific religious community in question, and on the assemblage of dominant and subordinated formations. For at least some of the social formations of religion, there are structural analogies to political ideas or movements that emerged throughout the history of mankind and that together cover almost the whole spectrum of possible political options. There is no necessity, but it may happen with some probability, that the dominance of one of these social formations within a religious community at a given time and place will result in a prevalence for the analogous political option.

Where the concept of a wider community of descent referring to common ancestors (formation 1) is dominant within a religious community, it is likely that the value system of the community will make a distinction between persons belonging to the legitimate offspring of the ancestors on the one hand and any other human person on the other hand. Outsiders may be considered inferior in one way or another. Analogous political options would be different forms of ethnocentrism or nationalism.[1]

Where the doctrine of a religious community highlights the idea of a cosmic order depending on the interplay between a divine ruler and his/her human representative (formation 3), the analogous political order would be a monarchic or autocratic system. Additionally, if the cosmologic concept of the religious community sees neighboring societies outside the monarchic rule as a threat to the cosmic order, there is some probability that the religious doctrine will be used to support forms of imperialism or colonialism.

Where within the overall value system of a religious community the idea of commonalities between all humankind is prevalent (formation 5), the analogous political ideas would be forms of universalism or internationalism. Political doctrines based on the equality of human rights (liberalism) or based on equal access to economic means (socialism, communism) could be likely political options related to such religious communities.

Considerations for the role of public theology

In the previous paragraphs it has been argued that religion does not qua religion display one specific social embodiment and that it does not qua religion have one specific political function. There are no qualities of social or political relevance that necessarily go along with a social entity being called a religion, and there are no qualities of social or political relevance

---

1 This refers to contexts where the nation state is more or less identified with an ethnic group, interpreting itself as a community of descent. In postcolonial contexts where the nation state has been defined by colonial powers irrespective of ethnic groups, a political movement rooted in a religious community of descent may rather be directed against the nation state.

that can be excluded for the same reason. Religion occurs in multiple social setups, and partly depending on the mix and priority of the different possible social formations, its involvement in the social and political realm can assume many different forms.

Along with these observations, it had to be stated that the social appearance of a religious community is not necessarily in line with what its authoritative texts and doctrines would suggest. If teachings and the production of knowledge maintain a dominant position within the overall social setup of a community, it may well be that the social reality of the community looks somehow similar to the community's own ideal concept of its social life. But the opposite is more likely: a sizeable difference between what the community envisions to be and what it actually embodies in social reality. To put it in Christian language: it is well possible that the visible church in some way mirrors the idea of the invisible church, but it is more likely that the visible church is quite different from the concept of the invisible church.

Nevertheless, the social embodiment of a religious community and the actions resulting from it will be what predominantly is perceived in the public sphere. No representative speaking for a religious community will be heard in public independent of what the social embodiment of the community already expresses. Public theology therefore is not in the position to make heard in public straight forward what it deems necessary to say on behalf of the religious community. Rather anything that theologians say in public will be heard in the context of the community's social body-language.

From this point of departure, it seems advisable that practitioners of public theology start with a critical analysis of the social formations and factors at work in their own community. This is even more true if public theology aims at serving a democratic and pluralistic society, as it is the common denominator of the contributions in this volume.

Among the six elementary social formations of religion, from which any given social embodiment of religion is assembled, there is not one specific formation that would be especially close to the political concept of democracy. Rather it may be stated that one of the social formations is especially remote from being compatible with democracy: religion functioning as an order of power (formation 3) that legitimizes the concentration of power in the hands of a divinely instituted ruler and a ruling class surrounding and supporting the ruler.

In democratic constitutions, political power is for good reasons not based on a divine institution but on the temporary delegation by the people. Democratic constitutions may refer to the responsibility towards God, but this is the opposite of what the divine institution of power has been throughout five millennia of political history: responsibility towards God is a limitation of human power referring to a greater horizon, whereas the concept of divinely instituted power expands the legitimation of power beyond human resources.

Therefore, the establishment of a democratic political system regularly will be accompanied by the abolition of concepts deriving the legitimacy of power directly from God – as far as such concepts have been in place beforehand. For the social embodiment of religion, a shift from divinely instituted monarchy to democracy brings about major transformations: the importance of the *order of power* (formation 3) within the overall social setup of the dominant religious community will be dismantled, and it will be replaced by other social formations. At the same time, the position of the so far dominant religious community within society will be challenged by other religious communities and by other worldviews, as the dominant religious community has lost its unique importance in providing the religious symbols legitimizing political power. Part of what we call "secularization" is nothing else than the effects of the abolition of divinely instituted monarchy on the social embodiment of religion. These effects do not take place instantly, but they rather imply long term transformations. In Germany, for example, the transformations evoked by the abolition of divinely instituted monarchy almost one hundred years ago have not yet been completed.

Along with or besides the incomplete transformation of religion accompanying the transition from divinely instituted monarchy to democracy, it may happen that religious symbols having once served the legitimacy of monarchic power will not be totally dismantled but rather transformed into symbols that provide a transcendent framing for democratic institutions or convictions. This phenomenon may be called "civil religion" – keeping in mind that the American political context where the term first has been employed (Bellah 1967) is different from the European context where almost every country has experienced the abolition of divinely instituted political power.

The critical evaluation of such civil religion may be one of the most important tasks for public theology, especially in the European context. Some aspects of civil religion may have their own right within democracy, for example to maintain the inviolability of human rights. But on the other hand, symbols belonging to an order of power justifying inequalities may live on in a democratic context, often in disguise. Especially symbolic orders maintaining discrimination based on racist or sexist assumptions, or discrimination of religious minorities, need to be looked at, and hidden remnants of imperial religion that continue to influence society after the transition to democracy need to be uncovered.

Public theology should critically examine religious symbols in light of democratic values, but it also has to analyze democratic institutions in light of religious values. Some religious traditions may well entail a potential to counterbalance shortcomings of democratic political systems, and public theology may be a suitable transmitter to make such traditions heard in democratic discourses. This especially may concern religious traditions from the two transcultural social formations of religion (formation 5 and 6).

Democratic states provide a political order granting equality to all citizens (at least in theory) – but they also limit equality in many respects to the boundaries of citizenship. The concept of human rights (again in theory) does not allow for such limitations – but the provisions made by democratic states to protect human rights in many ways distinguish between citizens and non-citizens. The European Union, for example, currently discriminates many people concerning their human right to find shelter from political persecution, cruelty, or violence, as for them there is no legal way to enter Europe in order to apply for shelter. People who do not have the necessary passport or money to get into Europe are left to live or die under the circumstances that are in reach for them. At present, it can be observed that democratic political systems are even especially vulnerable for initiatives to cut down the human rights of non-citizens, as political decisions not only depend on majorities, but even a minority of ten or twenty percent of the electorate can put political parties under such pressure that decisions augmenting the exclusion of non-citizens are taken according to the will of that minority.

The concept of all humanity belonging together as entailed in transcultural religious traditions has much in common with the concept of humanity as implied in the idea of human rights. Public theology may play an important role in political discourses by advocating the idea of all humanity belonging together against popular movements of xenophobia. Certainly, chances for this idea to be heard will be strengthened if the respective religious community is not only transcultural in theory but can empirically be perceived as a space of lived fellowship and mutual assistance by people irrespective of who they are and where they come from.

References

Bellah, Robert N. (1967): Civil Religion in America, *Daedalus: Journal of the American Academy of Arts and Sciences*, Vol. 96, 1–21.

Bourdieu, Pierre (1971): Genèse et structure du champ religieux, *Revue francaise de sociologie,* Vol. 12, No. 3, 295–334.

Durkheim, Émile (1912): *Les formes élementaires de la vie religieuse: le système totémique en Australie,* Paris: Alcan.

Feldtkeller, Andreas (2005): Grundtypen der Begründung von menschlicher Würde in der Religionsgeschichte, in: Wilfried Härle, Reiner Preul (eds.), *Menschenwürde*, Marburger Jahrbuch Theologie XVII, Marburg: N. G. Elwert, 25–47.

Feldtkeller, Andreas (2012): Kommunikationsstrukturen und Sozialformen von Religion, in: Michael Stausberg (ed.), *Religionswissenschaft*, Berlin: De Gruyter, 255–267.

Gombrich, Richard (1995): Sinn und Aufgabe des Sangha, in: Heinz Bechert, Richard Gombrich (eds.), *Der Buddhismus: Geschichte und Gegenwart,* München: C. H. Beck, 71–93.

Haynes, Jeffrey (ed.) (2010): *Routledge Handbook of Religion and Politics*, London: Routledge.

Joas, Hans (2006): Does Modernization Lead to Secularization? in: WRR (Scientific Council for Government Policy) (ed.), *Beyond the Separation between Church and State?*, WRR Lecture 2006, The Hague: WRR, 15–26.

Hempelmann, Reinhard (2006): *Religionen und Gewalt: Konflikt- und Friedenspotentiale in den Weltreligionen*, Göttingen: V&R unipress.

Kemp, Barry J. (1983): Old Kingdom, Middle Kingdom and Second Intermediate Period, c. 2686–1552 BC, in: B. G. Trigger, Barry J. Kemp, David O'Connor, Alan B. Lloyd, *Ancient Egypt: A Social History*, Cambridge: Cambridge University Press, 71–182.

Lössl, Josef (2010): *The Early Church: History and Memory*, London: T&T Clark International.

Markschies, Christoph (1999): *Between Two Worlds: Structures of Earliest Christianity*, London: SCM.

Martin, David (2005): *On Secularization: Towards a Revised General Theory*, Aldershot: Ashgate.

May, Fabienne (1986): *Les sépultures préhistoriques: Étude critique*, Paris: Presses du CNRS.

Müller-Karpe, Hermann (1998): *Grundzüge früher Menschheitsgeschichte*, Vol. I: *Von den Anfängen bis zum 3. Jahrtausend v. Chr.*, Darmstadt: Wissenschaftliche Buchgesellschaft.

Ohlig, Karl-Heinz (2002): *Religion in der Geschichte der Menschheit: Die Entwicklung des religiösen Bewusstseins*, Darmstadt: Wissenschaftliche Buchgesellschaft.

Riesebrodt, Martin, Konieczny, Mary E. (2010): Sociology of religion, in: John R. Hinnells (ed.), *The Routledge Companion to the Study of Religion*, 2nd ed., London: Routledge, 145–164.

Ritschl, Dietrich (1986): *The Logic of Theology,* transl. by J. Bowden, London: SCM.

Schneider, Tammi J. (2013): Assyrian and Babylonian Religions, in: Michele R. Salzman, Marvin A. Sweeney (eds.), *The Cambridge History of Religions in the Ancient World*, Vol. I: *From the Bronze Age to the Hellenistic Age*, Cambridge: Cambridge University Press, 54–83.

Weber, Max (1920): *Gesammelte Aufsätze zur Religionssoziologie*, Vol. I, Tübingen: J. C. B. Mohr (Paul Siebeck).

Wynne, Alexander (2015): *Buddhism. An Introduction*, London: I. B. Tauris

More than a Resource:
Covenant as a Basis for Societal Organization

Marcia Pally

Introduction

Of human thriving, the neurobiologist Darcia Narvaez writes, "To approach eudaimonia or human flourishing, one must have a concept of human nature, a realization of what constitutes a normal baseline, and an understanding of where humans are." (Narvaez 2014, 438) The Greeks thought similarly, as Thomas Nagel points out: one studies natural philosophy for the "religious" purpose of learning how the natural and human world works – the baseline in Narvaez's language – so as to live in harmony with it and so near eudaimonia (Nagel 2010, 3–4). The same may be said of government: we need an understanding of our baseline, how humans are, to design government that works with it for human flourishing.

This chapter is a prolegomenon to discussions of democracy. It looks at how humanity works so that we may develop government to suit. I shall propose that our "normal baseline" is relational as described by Aquinas and early Reformed political theorists as they drew on biblical notions of relationality and covenant. If our baseline is covenantal, we would have to account for this relationality in our political aims and means. I'll offer support for relationality from the sciences, which I'm happy to say are at last catching up to theology. I propose that developing political structures and economic policy in accord with human covenantality yields greater flourishing than the alternative; a few examples will be discussed. Making covenantal commitment understandable and *implementable* in the public sphere would be a substantial contribution of theology to politics, which is what this book is about.

Our relational "normal baseline"

Following Narvaez, we will start at the beginning: the human baseline is relational because Being is relational. Relation requires distinct entities, without which there is no inter-relating bond. The structure of existence, and thus human existence, is distinct entities amid relation. We know this from experience: even identical twins are distinct, different in character and worldview, yet all children develop in interaction with their physical and human surroundings. Each of us is a unique, separate being who becomes the unique person she is through relationship and interaction.

We know this also from theology. Being, exist-ability itself, results from the source of all that is. There could be nothing, but there's something. The source of all "something" is what some people call God (but for readers who find this unpersuasive, "source of all" suffices for the purposes of this chapter). Franz Rosenzweig called the source of all "the eventfulness of the limitless possibilities that will come to exist." (Wolfson 2014) After the kabbalist Ein Sof and F. W. J. Schelling, this source is not so much what precedes effects as what is realized as it yields effects. As existence results from this source, "God himself", Aquinas writes, "is properly the cause of universal being which is innermost in all things [beings] [...] in all things God works intimately." (Aquinas 1948) In Merleau-Ponty's words, divine "transcendence no longer hangs over man. He becomes, strangely, its privileged bearer." (Merleau-Ponty 1964, 71)

On one hand, particular beings are radically different from this source – differences in materiality/immateriality and finitude/infinitude. On the other, particulars intimately partake of the source of existence to exist at all. We partake of the source of existence – something radically *different* from ourselves – in order to exist. *This difference yet partaking/intimate relation is the way anything comes to be.* The grammar of existence is distinction-amid-relation. Kirk Wegter-McNelly summarizes, cosmos is "a place in which entangled independence-through-relationship is the fundamental characteristic of being." (Wegter-McNelly 2011, 136) The Trinity is a wonderful teacher of this idea. Each Trinitarian person is distinct, each with "its own particular distinguishing notes", as Gregory of Nyssa (1961, 207–209) wrote. Yet each is who he is through relation to other Trinitarian Persons (there is no "Father" without "Son" or "Spirit" without "Father" and "Son"). This idea of *perichoresis* (the Trinitarian Persons "dancing around" one another) allows Wegter-McNelly to continue, "The deity of this God resides not in the persons as distinct from one another but within and among the persons as they are related to one another, i.e., *in the relationality that constitutes* them and binds them." (Wegter-McNelly 2011, 128–129)[1]

1 Emphasis mine; Wegter-McNelly is building on Wolfhart Pannenberg, Sys-

Humanity, "in the image" of this relational God, partakes of his distinct-persons-in-community. It is a poetic way of saying that, as distinction-amid-relation is the source and grammar of exist-ability, all persons that exist are distinct from each other yet also in relation. There is no other way to be. Exist-ability as distinction-amid-relation makes humanity and society a matter of distinction-amid-relation. On one hand, we recall our distinct identical twins and the singularity of each person, yet on the other, "the individual is a fact of existence", Martin Buber wrote, "insofar as he steps into a living relation with other individuals." (Buber 1993, 203)

Distinction-amid-relation pertains also to our actions. Human action is radically different from the "acts" of the source of exist-ability, yet persons analogously, secondarily make things of what exists in world. In the classic example, God makes the laws of nature while persons plant seeds and make grains grow – what Aquinas calls the doctrine of "secondary causes". The medieval Muslim philosophers Al-Ash'ari and Al-Ghazali held that humanity "performs" what God creates. In the Judaic *tselem Elohim* (humanity made in the image of God), persons are radically different from incorporeal, imageless God. Yet we partake analogically of his imageless "image" (we partake of exist-ability). Such partaking enables humanity to act secondarily, within human abilities, to further God's vision for existence. Indeed, on this idea of "co-creatorship" we have the "moral correspondence" to do so, the *dmuth Elohim* (*similitudo*) to secondarily realize God's moral vision. Terence Fretheim (Fretheim 2005) explains, "Human beings are not only created in the image of God (this is who they are); they are also created to be the image of God (this is their role in the world)." Or as Karl Rahner (1966, 401—402) wrote, this is our "asymptotic" morality, our capacity to strive towards God's vision for existence.

Distinction-amid-relation: Support from the sciences

Exist-ability as distinction-amid-relation is not only a theological idea but a scientific one. The neuro-chemical pathways of the brain are not only genetically set but develop through each person's interactions with others. Narvaez again, "whom a person becomes is a co-construction of genes,

---

tematic theology. Vol. 1, trans. by G. W. Bromiley, Grand Rapids, MI: Eerdmans, 1991, 298, 323, 335.

gene expression from environmental effects [...] and the ecological and cultural surroundings [...] There is no being without shared social relations." (Narvaez 2014)[2] Evolutionary biology finds that we are a "hyper-cooperative species" (Schmid-Hempel 2015) in which "reciprocal altruism" (Trivers 1971, 35–57; Bowles & Ginties 2013) structures not only dyadic exchange and kin relations but large societal networks. It is the base also for interactions among highly mobile persons and groups *absent* long-term contact (Seyfarth & Cheney 2012). Evolutionary benefits to hunter-gatherer societies (95 percent of our evolutionary history) included improved hunting among cooperative rather than competitive clans and greater offspring survival as families helped each other with offspring. Nicholas Christakis and James Fowler find that, even amid present-day mobility and urban anonymity, generous acts prompt generous responses not only dyadically and immediately but expansively, in network fashion (Christakis & Fowler 2009). And we are not alone in this relational set-up. Primatologist Frans de Waal writes, "If one hyena or pelican were to monopolize all rewards, the system would collapse. Survival depends on sharing [...] chimpanzees and humans go even further by moderating their share of joint rewards to prevent frustration in others." (De Waal 2014, 71)

In short, we are not bound by the "selfish gene" but by relational ones. Post-quantum physics adds that humanity is relational *because* the grammar of existence is relational – an echo of the theology above. The trajectories of sub-atomic particles are "guided by" interactions with the trajectories of other particles. "We must accept the idea", physicist Carlo Rovelli writes, "that reality is only interaction [...] All things are continually interacting with one another, and in doing so each bears the traces of that with which it has interacted" (Rovelli 2016, 20, 69) even across hundreds of kilometers. Einstein's "spooky action at a distance" – relation at the quantum level – is how things are. Nobel Laureate Ilya Prigogine concludes that "communication" – even "consciousness" – is present in all chemical reactions, where molecules "know" and are affected by what the other molecules will do, again over significant distance. We are "embedded in a cooperating natural world." (Narvaez 2014, 429)

---

2 Daniel Stern identifies the "core self" and the "core self-with-another" in infants; see, Daniel N. Stern, The Interpersonal World of the Infant: A View from Psychoanalysis and Developmental Psychology, New York, NY: Basic Books, 2000.

Distinction-amid-relation: Expressed in covenant

The world of reciprocal impact that we live in entails reciprocal responsibility. For the world's relational set-up to work, each distinct person – dependent on others for survival and development – must attend to those on whom she is dependent as others must attend to her. The name for this reciprocal commitment is covenant.

Covenant is a bond between distinct parties where each party gives for the sake and flourishing of the other. However profound the covenant, it does not subsume the person, nor is the individual sacrifice-able for the group or for covenant itself (the point of the binding of Isaac narrative). In Lenn Goodman's words, "The covenant itself [...] rests on (and thus cannot create) the freedom of the covenantors." (Goodman 1991, 41–42)

In the Judaic tradition, the source of human covenantality is twofold. We partake of the distinction-amid-relation grammar of existence (we are in the image of a relational, covenantal God) *and* we are in covenantal relation with him.

Covenants of reciprocal commitment among equals are easily imagined, as are covenants with asymmetric terms between unequal parties. The innovation of the Hebrew Bible is reciprocity between unequals, between the divine and human and among persons of different status. In this reciprocity, stipulative features might arise (as parents stipulate that a child cleans her room), but covenant is not stipulative in motive or *telos* (one doesn't have children so that they clean their rooms). Unlike stipulative contract, which protects interests, covenant protects relationship. Where breach of contract generally voids the bond, covenant is irrevocable (one doesn't cancel covenant if children fail to clean their rooms).

One aspect of God's covenant with humanity, as we've seen, is co-creatorship. In covenant, God entrusts humanity to further his vision for existence in world. Another aspect is the inauguration and maintenance of covenant by gift, often of an item of little economic value. As, among others, Marcel Mauss and Lewis Hyde have observed (Mauss 1990; Hyde 1983), the allegiance – the *spirit* – of the donor is given to the donee in the performative act of gift-giving. Donation of spirit makes the bond. It begins dyadically between God and Adam: God breaths his "spirit" (*nishmat cha'im*, Genesis 2:7) into Adam. Also dyadically, God gives Noah life and covenant; Noah and his children return the gift in performing the seven Noahite moral laws. God gives to the patriarchs the gifts of covenant and land, of survival in world. In reciprocity, their children return the harvest of the land to the Temple. Returning tokens of the harvest to God is not sustenance of the infinite transcendent (who needs nothing) but acceptance of the reciprocity of covenant.

Yet covenant does not remain dyadic. Persons give to God, in Judaic tradition, also by giving in charity, *hekdesh* (made holy). In this triangulation, one gives to God by giving to a third party, persons in need. These relations-of-giving are mutually constitutive: covenantal commitment to others constitutes covenant with God, and covenant with God sustains us in covenantal commitments to others.

Covenant – reciprocal commitment – thus extends from dyad to larger associations. Reciprocal gift becomes gift exchange network, as Mauss described it, where gift from *God to person* generates gift *from person to neighbor* and on to the next person through the giving loop, thus sustaining it (cf. Godbout & Caillé 1998). There is some argument that gift-exchange networks aren't possible absent the physical proximity of pre-modern communities. But covenantal gift-exchange networks were sustained across infrequent contact and vast distances (thousands of miles of the Pacific, for instance). Modern societies, with airplanes, Skype, Instagram, etc., cannot claim impossible what was done in canoes.

We find the triangulated covenant (from God to person to other persons) in the Ten Commandments, the first three of which pertain to person and God, the rest, among persons. In Numbers 5:6, harm to persons, abrogating covenant with them, abrogates covenant with God.[3] Amos and Proverbs denounce the hypocrisy of performing rituals while abandoning the afflicted, as if one could maintain bond with God absent bond with the needy[4] – one of the most oft-repeated of biblical and rabbinic ideas.

In the Second Testament, the triangulation of covenantal commitment is seen in the famous passage in 1 John 4:20, "For whoever does not love their brother and sister, whom they have seen, cannot love God, whom they have not seen." Absent love of others, there is no love of God. But John continues: love of God enables love of others, "We love because he first loved us" (1 John 4:19). Irenaeus echoes, "to love Him above all, and one's neighbor […] do reveal one and the same God." (Irenaeus 1989,

3 "Any man or woman who wrongs another in any way *and so* is unfaithful to the Lord is guilty."

4 Amos 5:21-24: "I hate, I despise your religious festivals; your assemblies are a stench to me … But let justice roll on like a river, righteousness like a never-failing stream"; Proverbs 21:3: "To do what is right and just is more acceptable to the Lord than [ritual] sacrifice."

478) Or as Augustine put it, the "relic" of a covenant-making God in each person gives her the capacity to love other persons covenantally.

But here something is added. In the Judaic tradition, the source of humanity's covenantality is twofold: being in the image of a covenantal God and being in covenant with him. In Christian tradition, the source is threefold; the third source is the triune nature of the divine. As the Christian God is triune, the "relic" of God in each person is triune, too – this is the covenantal relationality of the Trinity. This relationality within each of us, endowing us with relationality, enables us to love others in covenant. All in all, God makes to humanity a triune gift in covenant: the gift of Being itself, of being in God's (relational, covenantal) image, and the gift of himself in Jesus. Yet Jesus is not any gift (like an inert object); he is the gift of relationality, love, and covenant itself. He demonstrates covenantal relationality in world; we may learn it and extend it to others.

In sum, humanity, made in God's (relational, covenantal) image, is given relational, covenantal Being and *a* relational being in covenant (Jesus). Thus, we have the capacity, *dmuth Elohim* or *similitudo*, to respond to God and others covenantally. This capacity, Catherine Keller writes, is what it means to be "response-able".

As covenantal commitment is triangulated from God to person to other persons, which persons are in the loop? Consistent with the idea that the set-up of exist-ability per se is relational/covenantal, the biblical answer is: all the nations.[5] The covenant to all three patriarchs is "for the blessing of all the nations" (Genesis 12:3, 26:4, 28:14). God makes covenants with non-Israelites as all persons, made in God's image, are capable of "moral correspondence", of acting morally and committing themselves to covenantal bonds. Covenantal commitment undergirds the extensive biblical[6] and rabbinic obligations to the needy and stranger. So extensive are those for the stranger that they are cited as a model for treatment of the Hebrew poor (Leviticus 25:35-39, Leviticus 17-26). Ezekiel 47:22-23 grants strangers even land rights. The effectiveness of these commitments prodded the Emperor Julian to demand improvement in Roman poor relief: "it is disgraceful that, when no Jew ever has to beg, and the impious Gali-

5 One could invent an exclusionary covenant, commitment only to and within one's own group, but it would not be grounded in the ontology of the Jewish and Christian traditions.

6 A brief sampling: Exodus 21:2, Exodus 22:25-27, Leviticus 25:4-6, 13, Deuteronomy 14:22, Deuteronomy 15:1-2, 7-9, 12-15, Deuteronomy 23:15-16, 19, Deuteronomy 24:19-22.

laeans support not only their own poor but ours as well, all men see that our people lack aid from us." (Stern 1980, 549–550)

The enemy too must be approached covenantally, with a request for a peace settlement before the commencement of any war (Deuteronomy 20:10). Residents of besieged cities, on the rabbinic, Maimonidean, and Nachmonidean view, must be allowed to leave unharmed. Enemy nations may not be oppressed even when at war with them (2 Chron. 28:8-15). Truces and peace agreements must be honored even if the enemy breaches them (Joshua 9). A scorched earth policy is prohibited, and captives must be provided for.[7] Even the enslaving Egyptians are to be welcomed into the family nations and granted this regard after the third generation post-Exodus.

The medieval period gives us one of the most soaring expressions of the triangulated covenant. The great French commentator Rashi reads in Isaiah, "I cannot be God unless you are my witness", and Rashi glosses, "I am the God who will be whenever you bear witness to love and justice in the world." God can be God when persons are loving and just to each other. Levinas builds on this idea: relationship with God, he writes, "can be traced back to the love of one's neighbor." (Levinas 1994, 146–147) The Catholic theologian Richard Kearney evocatively reprises, "This is a *deus capax* who in turn calls out to the *homo capax* of history in order to be made flesh, again and again – each moment we confront the face of the other, welcome the stranger." Echoing both Levinas and Rashi, Kearney concludes that "welcoming the stranger" is the site of our bond with God, "A capacitating God who is capable of all things cannot actually be or become incarnate until we say yes." (Kearney 2009, 143,155)

We, in God's image, are set up as distinct persons, each in covenantal relation to God and others. Until we say "yes" to the covenantal commitment, God works in world and waits.

7 Sifre Bemidbar 157 s.v. Vayishlach otam (on Numbers 31:7); Maimonides, The Laws of Kings (Hilchot Melachim) 6:4; see also Nachmanides, Additions to Sefer Hamitzvot, Mitzvah 5, where he mandates that one "behave well in war even with enemies at the time of war."

Covenant as political theory: The Reformed tradition and early America

In considering the role of covenant in human arrangements, Yoram Hazony begins from the idea that covenantal commitment is the structure of our existence. The Bible, he writes, is "a philosophical argument for the importance of Israel's covenant with God not only for the Jews but also for 'all the nations of the earth.' […] [The biblical author] wished to persuade his readers that there exists a law whose force is of a universal nature, because it derives from the way the world itself was made." (Hazony 2012, 22, 249)

That it is covenantal relationality – and not some other ontology – which structures our existence grounds several Christian traditions as well, among them Catholic Social Teaching and important aspects of early Protestant development. The peasant revolts of the 1520s were grounded on the idea that society is covenantly based and thus that gross inequalities between elites and commoners are unsupportable (Brecht 1974; Blickle 1987). Many Reformed thinkers deemed covenant the foundation and form of society. They saw a "symbiosis" between the divine bonds (among Trinitarian persons, between God and humanity) and human bonds (McCoy & Baker 1991, 52). Thus, *analogous to the bonds of the Trinitarian Persons* and *analogous to covenant between God and humanity, each (distinct) person in God's (relational) image is responsible for maintaining covenantal commitment with God and among persons.* Among persons, covenant binds the family, church, and guild, which in turn make up the larger covenanted networks of town and nation. It is these covenantal commitments that each person must support.

The spring-board thinker of Reformed covenantal politics, Heinrich Bullinger, was principle author of the First Helvetic Confession (1536) and author of the Second (1566). He traced covenant from God and Adam to the Judaic patriarchs, which he held is the same triangulated covenant as taught by Jesus and Paul (Bullinger 1534, 119). Not all Reformed thinkers agreed; Calvin held to two covenants (the "carnal" or law covenant of Israel and the spiritual covenant of Christianity), and his doctrine of double pre-destination gave covenantal *reciprocity* to God smaller importance. However, others like Cornelius Wiggertz followed Bullinger in holding to one reciprocating covenant through the ages and testaments.

Wiggertz was a source for Arminian theology and its accent on humanity's capacity, by prevenient (this worldly) grace, to reciprocate God's love and act morally, with covenantal regard, toward God and others. As John Wesley, the eighteenth-century advocate of Arminianism in England and

America, later would write, "God worketh in you, therefore you *can* work [...] God worketh in you; therefore you *must* work; you must be 'workers together with him' (they are the very words of the Apostle); otherwise, he will cease working" (see, *On Working Out Our Own Salvation*). Zacharias Ursinus was more emphatic, holding that God made a covenant with humanity at creation and offers salvation to all of faith and moral conduct (not only to particular confessions; see, Major Catechism, 1561/1562). Kaspar Olevianus, Ursinus's colleague in Heidelberg, went further, holding that covenantal commitment was not with humanity *at* creation but rather *with* creation, structuring not only human relations but world itself.

Among the first to develop an explicitly covenantal political theory was Johannes Althusius. Persons individually, he held, are created helpless but have a "symbiotic" relational nature *so that* they live in covenantal commitment with God and each other (Althusius 1964). Politics is the art of creating worldly covenantal structures, "the art of associating (*consociandi*) men for the purpose of establishing, cultivating, and conserving social life among them", including institutions, policies, mores, and a division of power so that society proceeds covenantally, without concentration or abuse. The "fundamental law" of the nation or commonwealth "is nothing other than certain covenants (*pacta*) by which many cities and provinces come together and agree to establish and defend one and the same commonwealth by common work, counsel, and aid."

Contra political theorist Jean Bodin – who held that nations are guaranteed not by human *pacta* but by indivisible, eternal sovereignty vested in a prince – Althusius declared that sovereignty lies in the *network* of covenantal bonds. While magistrates may administer, "It is not a collection of individuals but a covenanted whole that has the rights of sovereignty." (McCoy & Baker 1991, 60) The "moral" law of the Ten Commandments is the core of covenantal responsibility, which is interpreted into "proper laws" specific to each community. Should a magistrate or prince violate covenantal responsibility with God or community, Althusius held (*contra* Bodin and unusually for his time), they may be removed from office.

This foreshadowing of representative government consented to by the covenanted community was elaborated by Johannes Cocceius, born the year of the publication of Althusius' *Politics* (1603) and dying the year of the Fundamental Constitution of Carolina (1669), written by the great sponsor of covenantal politics, John Locke. Like Bullinger, Cocceius held to one covenant of love and community within the Triune God, between God and humanity, and among persons. One comes to understand this covenant, he held, by reading Scripture within an interpreting community.

Because we are in the image of a relational, covenantal God *and* in covenant with him, human covenant reflects covenant with God. Thus we may come to understand bond with God through covenantal life with others, notably the covenanted church community of Bible readers.

Cocceius recognized that, as persons live and study Scripture in varying communities and circumstances, each understands it differently, a perspective that adumbrates Kant's critic Johann Georg Hamann and Romantics such as Herder and Schleiermacher as well as later social science. Multiple interpretations of Scripture, Cocceius held, will emerge as God works differently in different contexts. The process is creative and evolving under God's vision, in which God and humanity participate. (We hear echoes of Jewish "co-creatorship", which Cocceius had learned in his studies of Hebrew and rabbinics; one might note also a distant, family resemblance to Hegel's World Historical Spirit.) Without multiple interpretations, Cocceius wrote, the Bible would become irrelevant in the face of new conditions. "There is no law that orders the person who comes after to be content with the things his predecessors have learned."[8] (McCoy & Baker 1991, 76) Resistance to variety and change is, on Cocceius' account, pride and fallenness as it presumes one interpretation is absolute truth, which only God can know.

Here we find intimations of the Enlightenment proposal that human knowledge, as imperfect, benefits from varying perspectives, an idea that contributed to notions of freedom of expression, association, and press. Over the following century, the Reformed view of covenant saw effects in Germany, England, Scotland, and the American colonies. The Mayflower Compact (1620) declares the new Massachusetts colony a covenant of persons bound together as they are bound to God: "We, whose names are underwritten [...] solemnly and mutually in the Presence of God and one another, covenant and combine ourselves together into a civil Body Politick." (Mayflower Compact 1620) Althusius' and Cocceius' themes are all present: the New World would be part of the covenantal-historical process, guided by God and implemented by men in free covenant with him and each other. Laws are developed by the governed for the common good as guided by God's principles.

A decade later, John Winthrop declared in *A Model of Christian Charity* that his Massachusetts community hangs together by bonds to each other and God. His understanding of society is Althusius' anthropology: "*so*

8 In his Summa theologiae ex scrituris repetita.

that every man might have need of others, and from hence they might be all knit more nearly together in the Bonds of brotherly affection." These bonds constitute the sovereign group, and in them "we must love one another with a pure heart fervently. We must bear one another's burdens." Thus, in community governance, "the care of the public must over-sway all private respects, by which, not only conscience, but mere civil policy, doth bind us." (Winthrop 1630, 34–35) As Althusius had specified, political representatives were legitimate only as long as they governed covenantally. When the magistrates of Massachusetts Bay tried to make themselves into a permanent body, granting themselves power over the covenanted community, the citizens responded with term limits. To ensure that the covenanted community was preserved and that no power overtakes it, the Body of Liberties was enacted in 1641, with many of its provisions later written into the U.S. Bill of Rights.

At the end of the century, John Locke's *Two Treatises on Governmen*t and *A Letter Concerning Toleration* synthesized the covenantal literature on church and state. Church, for Locke, is a covenanted body which men enter freely, out of love for its precepts and each other. "A church, then, I take to be a voluntary society of men, joining themselves together of their own accord in order to the public worshipping of God." Locke followed Cocceius in recognizing the plurality of scriptural interpretations as God works differently in different worldly conditions. Thus, as no one can be sure of the absolute truth of an idea, none may be persecuted for holding unpopular ones. State, Locke held, is too a covenanted body, "a society of men constituted only for the procuring, preserving, and advancing their own civil interests." (Locke 1698) Thus, both church and state are compacts: one for spiritual matters, which may not be settled by human sanctions, the other for civil flourishing, which may require sanctions by community representatives should covenantal commitment be violated.

The U.S. Declaration of Independence (1776) relies on Althusius' and Locke's idea that sovereigns may be deposed for covenant violations (and on Locke's specific criteria for doing so). The Virginia Declaration of Rights (1776), forerunner of the U.S. Bill of Rights, declares, as Althusius might have done, "That all power is vested in, and consequently derived from, the people […] That government is, or ought to be, instituted for the common benefit." (Virginia Declaration of Rights 1776) Covenantal thinking also undergirds the opening affirmation of the U.S. Constitution, that government is by "We the People" in compact with each other (1787/1789). American Constitutional protections of freedom of religion (1789) are rooted in Cocceius' and Locke's recognition of the plurality of

Scriptural interpretation. The division of government into three branches and into federal and state powers follows covenantal principles of checks and balances to shield the covenanted community from tyranny and abuse.

Covenant as a basis for present politics: A few examples

As covenant pre-supposes distinct persons giving for the sake and flourishing of others, it pre-empts self-absorption, greed, and abandonment, replacing them with concern for the common good – the *foedus* (covenant) and *demos*. Covenant does not recede from the needs and plans of individuals but sees them *not* as a competitive zero-sum game: me-first, my firm, market share, or party. Rather, as the biologists tell us, individual goals and concerns develop in relation with those of others, and so each must account for others in a network of reciprocal commitments for a future understood also as shared.

Reciprocal, covenantal commitments are not a codex but, as Cocceius noted, a process of reciprocal learning and discussion – both when common needs and goals are evident and when we are beset by conflict. This process requires, in Joel Hunter's marvelous words, asking as a *first* step "why the other side is for the other side" (Hunter 2008, 84–85) and brokering the answers into mores, policy, and institutions. We may begin with near others, but given the present mobility of persons, goods, microbes, and ideas, arenas of reciprocal impact and responsibility may reach across the globe. Though touted as the guru of greed, Adam Smith proposed just this: in markets as in all of society, he wrote, each should "endeavour, as much as he can, to put himself in the situation of the other, and to bring home to himself every little circumstance of distress which can possibly occur to the sufferer." (Smith 1976, 21)

Politically, a covenantal mindset (asking "why the other side is for the other side") would strengthen the power of democratically self-governing institutions – local and regional government; labor unions; industry, trade, and professional associations; grassroots political groups; faith-based organizations – so that they and the individuals they represent can work out policy alongside national government and the market. It would mean building into political processes the fora for such groups to work *regularly* with each other. This stands in contrast to each group confronting others only at crisis points, when animus is present and trusting ways of working together are not developed. It contrasts also with a situation in which each group speaks individually with government and so, not hearing the variety of aims and problems around the table, may persist in its own perspective rather than work the concerns of all into the compromise that is policy and practice.

Economically, a covenantal worldview will not change market relations (supply and demand, etc.) but will change relations within the market, prioritizing them and our reciprocal responsibility. It will alter economic transactions by configuring them within mutual regard and common goals. Today, this might entail: improved education; worker re-training in "old industry" areas; regional re-development coordinated among local and national governments and business, notably firms that close factories. The case of Pittsburgh is illustrative: its loss of 5,100 iron and steel jobs over 25 years was outstripped by redevelopment gains of 66,000 new jobs in health care, banking, and professional services (Irwin 2016). Other proposals include tying management earnings to long-term development rather than short-term profits, more progressive taxation, and repealing tax loopholes that allow transnational corporations to pay far less tax than the official rate or, if they move to tax havens, to pay little tax at all.[9] In the U.S., Democrat-voting states have substantially more of this investment and progressive taxation than Republican-voting states and score higher on income, life expectancy, and education levels.[10]

Concluding remarks

If these are not good suggestions, others will be better. But the proposal here has been covenant as framework and bulwark for governmental systems based on the consent and voice of the governed.

One might note that such a covenantal worldview is not much present. But worldviews change, as they did from monarchical to democratic views of sovereignty. Moreover, the short sketch of covenantal political theory suggests that grounding societal organization on covenantal commitment would not be a change to something new but the resurrection of the first modern developments in democracy.

9 http://www.nytimes.com/interactive/2016/12/16/business/economy/nine-new-findings-about-income-inequality-piketty.html?emc=eta1.

10 http://www.nytimes.com/2016/07/31/opinion/campaign-stops/the-path-to-prosperity-is-blue.html?emc=edit_ty_20161229&nl=opinion-today&nlid=64605949&te=1

If we have lost sight of them, we have lost sight of our "baseline" as distinct persons who become who we are in relation and so must *see to* those relations in reciprocal commitment. Anthropologists Nancy Abrams and Joel Primack write, "We have no sense of how we and our fellow humans fit into the big picture [...] Without a big picture we are very small people." (Abrams & Primack 2012, xi–xii)

In public discussions of the role of religion in democratic society, most frequent is the "charity/social service" discourse. Theology, on this account, exists to provide good works when the market won't and the state can't. I'd aim for something bigger. The covenantal theology described here anchors us in the relational conditions of Being and of human beings so that we may build culture and politics upon them for shared human flourishing.

References

Abrams, Nancy, Primack, Joel (2012): *The New Universe and the Human Future*, New Haven, CT: Yale University Press.

Althusius, Johannes (1964): *The politics of Johannes Althusius. An abridged translation of the third edition of politica methodice digesta, atque exemplis sacris et profanis illustrate*, transl. by F. Carney, Boston, MA: Beacon Press. Retrieved from http://www.constitution.org/alth/alth.htm. (Original work published 1603), Chapters 1, 3–4.

Aquinas, Thomas (1948): *Summa Theologica* 1–5, trans. by Fathers of the Dominican English Province, Westminster, MD: Christian Classics, Ia, q. 105, art. 5.

Blickle, Peter (ed.) (1987): *Zugänge zur bäuerlichen Reformation*, Zurich: Chronos.

Bowles, Samuel, Ginties, Herbert (2013): *A Cooperative Species: Human Reciprocity and Its Evolution,* Princeton, NJ: Princeton University Press.

Brecht, Martin (1974): Der theologische Hintergrund der Zwölf Artikel der Bauernschaft in Schwaben, *Zeitschrift für Kirchengeschichte*, Vol. 85, 174–208.

Buber, Martin (1993): *Between Man and Man*, New York, NY: Routledge.

Bullinger, H. (1534): A brief exposition of the one and eternal testament or covenant of God, in: Charles McCoy, J. Wayne Baker (eds.), *Fountainhead of federalism: Heinrich Bullinger and the covenantal tradition,* Louisville, KY: Westminster/John Knox Press 1991 (original work published 1534).

Christakis, Nicholas, Fowler, James (2009): *Connected: The Surprising Power of Our Social Networks and How They Shape Our Lives – How Your Friends' Friends' Friends Affect Everything You Feel, Think, and Do*, New York, NY: Little, Brown & Company.

De Waal, Frans (2014): One for All, *Scientific American*, No. 311, September 2014.

Fretheim, Terence E. (2005): *God and World in the Old Testament: A Relational Theology of Creation*, Nashville, TN: Abignon Press, Kindle location 1294–1295.

Godbout, Jacques, Caillé, Alain (1998): *The World of the Gift*, trans. by Donald Winkler, Montreal: McGill-Queen's University Press.

Goodman, Lenn E. (1991): *On Justice: An Essay in Jewish Philosophy*, New Haven, CT: Yale University Press.

Gregory of Nyssa: Ad petrium, in: Roy J. Deferrari, trans., *Saint Basil: The Letters II*, London: Loeb Classical Library. Heinemann, 1961, Epp. 197–227.

Hazony, Yoram (2012): *The Philosophy of Hebrew Scripture*, Cambridge: Cambridge University Press.

Hunter, Joel C. (2008): *A New Kind of Conservative*, Ventura, CA: Gospel Light Publishing.

Hyde, Lewis (1983): *The Gift: Imagination and the Erotic Life of Property,* New York, NY: Vintage Books.

Irenaeus (1989): *Against heresies [Adversus haereses]*, ed. Alexander Roberts and James Donaldson, Grand Rapids, MI: Eerdmans, 180 CE.

Irwin, Neil (2016): Donald Trump's Economic Nostalgia, *The New York Times* 28/06/2016, http://www.nytimes.com/2016/06/29/upshot/donald-trumps-economic-nostalgia.html?em_pos=large&emc=edit_nn_20160629&nl=morning-briefing &nlid=64605949 (accessed Apr 7th, 2017).

Kearney, Richard (2009): Paul's Notion of Dunamis: Between the Possible and the Impossible, in: John Caputo, Linda Alcoff (eds.), *St. Paul Among the Philosophers*, Bloomington & Indianapolis, IN: Indiana University Press, 142–159.

Levinas, Emmanuel (1994): Revelation in the Jewish Tradition, in: *Beyond the Verse: Talmudic Readings and Lectures*, trans. by G. Mole, Bloomington: Indiana University Press.

Locke, John (1698): *Letter concerning toleration*, retrieved from http://www.let.rug.nl/usa/documents/1651-1700/john-locke-letter-concerning-toleration-1689.php.

Mauss, Marcel (1990): *The Gift: The Form and Reason for Exchange in Archaic Society,* trans. by W. D. Halls, London, UK: Routledge.

Mayflower Compact (1620), retrieved from http://www.let.rug.nl/usa/documents/1600-1650/mayflower-compact-1620.php.

McCoy, Charles, Baker, J. Wayne (1991): *Fountainhead of federalism: Heinrich Bullinger and the covenantal tradition,* Louisville, KY: Westminster/John Knox Press.

Merleau-Ponty: Maurice (1964): *Signs*, trans. by Richard McCleary, Evanston, IL: Northwestern University Press.

Nagel, Thomas (2010): Secular Philosophy and the Religious Temperament, in: Thomas Nagel, *Secular Philosophy and the Religious Temperament*, Oxford: Oxford University Press.

Narvaez, Darcia (2014): *Neurobiology and the Development of Human Morality: Evolution, Culture, and Wisdom*, New York: W. W. Norton & Company.

Rahner, Karl (1966): The Theology of Power, in: Karl Rahner, *Theological Investigations*, Vol. 4, London, UK: Darton Longman & Todd.

Rovelli, Carlo (2016): *Seven Brief Lessons on Physics*, New York: Penguin Publishing.

Schmid-Hempel, Paul (2015): Institute for integrative biology, Zurich, Switzerland, personal communication, May 15, 2015.

Seyfarth, Robert, Cheney, Dorothy (2012): The Evolutionary Origins of Friendship, *Annual Review of Psychology*, Vol. 63, 179–199.

Smith, Adam (1976): *The Theory of Moral Sentiments*, eds. D. Raphael and A. Macfie, Oxford: Clarendon Press, 1976 (originally published 1759).

Stern, Menahem (1980): *Greek and Latin Authors on Jews and Judaism. From Tacitus to Simplicius,* Jerusalem: Israel Academy of Sciences and Humanities, No. 482.

Trivers, Robert (1971): The Evolution of Reciprocal Altruism, *The Quarterly Review of Biology*, Vol. 46, No. 1, 35–57.

Virginia Declaration of Rights (1776), retrieved from http://www.let.rug.nl/usa/documents/1776-1785/the-virginia-declaration-of-rights-1776.php.

Wegter-McNelly, Kirk (2011): *The Entangled God: Divine Relationality and Quantum Physics*, New York, NY: Routledge.

Winthrop, John (1630): *A modell of Christian charity*, Collections of the Massachusetts historical society (Boston, 3rd series, 1838), 7:31–48, retrieved from http://history.hanover.edu/texts/winthmod.html.

Wolfson, Elliot R. (2014): *Giving Beyond the Gift: Apophasis and Overcoming Theomania*, New York, NY: Fordham University Press, Kindle location 2812

Public Theology and Democracy:
A Muslim Perspective

Mouez Khalfaoui

Regardless of its specific definition and interpretations[1], democracy is currently considered to be the most adaptable concept to achieve secure political participation and the best guarantee for transparent governance of social and economic affairs. Accordingly, nearly the majority of societies in our contemporary world have adopted it.[2] Notwithstanding, the interpretation and implementation of this doctrine vary greatly within different contexts and have visibly contrasting outcomes.[3] The events of the last five years in several Muslim countries have consistently shed light on processes of democratization in that region. This paper addresses how democracy has been interpreted and implemented in the Islamic world in past and present, with specific focus on the position of Muslim theologians regarding democracy. The paper ends with a discussion on the current issue of coupling Islam and democracy in Western Europe.

In this paper, I argue that democracy has been continuously debated in the Muslim world from the 19th century onward. The concept of democracy meant here is mainly the Western understanding of democracy, i.e. the notion that accompanied the birth of nation states in Europe. Over the last

1 The *Cambridge Dictionary* defines "democracy" quite broadly so that it can accommodate any addition and interpretation: "The belief in freedom and equality between people, or a system of government based on this belief, in which power is either held by elected representatives or directly by the people themselves." Online edition available at: http://dictionary.cambridge.org/de/worterbuch/englisch/democracy (accessed Feb. 19th, 2017).

2 The classical distinction between «the democratic states" and the rest of the world is no longer accepted as valid by the scientific and academic community, as the majority of states is at least nominally democratic either in their constitutions or elsewhere contained in their written doctrines. This does not mean that all share the same understanding of democracy.

3 It is self-evident that the majority of political regimes worldwide make reference to democracy either in how they choose to name their states, in their constitutions, or in other forms. This indicates that democracy is held in a generally positive light.

centuries, this concept has undergone two contradictory interpretations in the Islamic world. In the first period (from mid-19th to mid-20th century), democracy was principally appreciated and interpreted almost exclusively by Muslim elites. It is therefore not surprising that those elites tried to introduce it into the political and social life sometimes by force and without any understanding of the population, who were not sufficiently prepared for such a concept. However, from approximately the 1970's onward, democracy experienced an extensive appreciation among Muslim populations and became the rallying cry of the masses throughout the Islamic world. While Muslim governing elites are still invested in presenting themselves as the incarnation of democracy and its advocate, there exist other understandings of democracy which were and are still embraced by the masses. This latter notion of democracy is thought to be a popular egalitarian concept, therefore used to be considered as "genuine" democracy. The divergence between these two understandings of democracy has always resulted in clashes and uprisings in many parts of the Islamic world. This paper will show how these two concepts of democracy have emerged and developed and which role theology played in this regard. To illustrate the latter point, I will present various case studies from different Islamic countries.

1. Muslim theologians and democracy in the 19th century

It is without question that Muslim theologians were among the first group of intellectuals in the Islamic world to debate the concept of democracy. They conceived of it as the best method of governance worth importing from the West to the Islamic states. As late as the middle of the 19th century, Muslim theologians returned to the idea of democracy whenever they took up the question of how to improve and to reform the Islamic world. They debated democracy in the framework of reform and modernization which were and continue to be among the main subjects of intellectual debates in the Islamic world. Muslim theologians often draw a comparison between the underdeveloped Islamic world and powerful Western countries (Sharabi 1970, 44). Their main question is how the West managed to become developed and why the Islamic world had become underdeveloped and could not help itself to get out of its ever-worsening situation (Tarabischi 2000, 39). During the 19th century, there were two main tendencies among Muslim theologians. On the one hand, there existed those who were still convinced by the Islamic classical way of governance and leadership based on the principal of the *Khilafa* (Qureshi 1999, 34). The representative figures of this group are Jamal Din al Afghani (d. 1897) and Muhammad Abduh (d. 1905) (Sharabi 1970, 4). They reduced Western supremacy to technological advancements and saw only this aspect as being worth importing. They rejected the supremacy of the West in terms of moral issues and continue to think of the validity and legitimacy of Islamic values (ibid., 50). The second group consisted of those who were convinced of the fact that Western wealth and power was not limited to technological and military capabilities but also encompassed the doctrines of governance and leadership. This group was inspired by the Western concepts of democracy and governance; its proponents wanted to implement these concepts in their countries and looked for justifications in the Muslim founding texts. The cases of Kheyreddine Pasha from Tunisia (1810–1890) and Abdurrahman al Kawakibi (d. 1902) from Syria illustrate this issue.

Kheyreddine Pasha lived in a period in which the Tunisian dynasty, still under the thumb of the Ottoman Empire, was suffering from economic, social, and political underdevelopment (Magdalena 2014). Kheyreddine had been appointed the head of different ministries and institutions to help develop them. He was interested in improving the conditions of the dynasty in Tunisia and those of the population. He was aware of the danger approaching from the outside in the form of the French colonial power; France had already colonized Algeria and was trying to expand its power over Tunisia. He also tried to conceive of ways how to solve illiteracy, hunger, and social underdevelopment. Kheyreddine tried to adopt the concept of Western way of governance. His interpretation of democracy is one of the first in the Islamic world at that time. His knowledge of Western methods of governance was mainly based on his visits to European countries, especially to France, where he spent more than four years in which he was able to closely experience and examine the inner workings of democracy. Kheyreddine wrote a leading book of political history entitled *The simplest way to recognize the situation in the kingdoms* (*'aqwam al masālik fi ma'rifat 'ahwāl al mamālik)* (Al Tounsi 2012). Kheyreddine drafted this in an era when politics and theology were still closely related to each other within the political system of the Islamic world. Accordingly, theology was the main lens through which to gain understanding. Therefore, the book retains a theological focus, and his discussion on democracy demonstrates that Kheyreddine tried to explain to his interlocutors[4], who were mainly politicians, that Sharia and Islamic thought still have the same and equal values of good governance as those shared by the European common wisdom (ibid., 101). To illustrate his ideas, Kheyreddine describes how European institutions, such as ministries, hospitals, and other administrations in France, Germany, Russia, England, and many other European states and monarchies, function and how the liberal democratic way of governance achieves prosperity in these countries.[5]

The contribution of Kheyreddine to the debate on democracy in the Islamic world at that time consists of the fact that he reflects the spirit of his time. He also demonstrates the impact of Islamic theology on the debate on Western values in that it was impossible to think of democracy outside a religious framework. For this reason, Kheyreddine attempted time and again to explain that genuine democracy is not in contradiction with Islamic theology and that adopting this ideology wouldn't present any threat to Islam (Al Tounsi 2012, 19). The failure of Kheyreddine in Tunisia and later on in Istanbul to get his innovative concepts implemented is the proof of the fact that Muslim theologians and stakeholders of the 19th century were unable to adopt the Western concepts of democracy and governance without facing harsh rejection.

Another 19th century Muslim theologian who faced deportation and rejection because of his opinion was al-Kawakibi, who penned *The Nature of Despotism* (*Tabā'i' al Istibdād wa maṣāri' al Isti'bād*) (2011). Al Kawakibi (d. 1902) was a major figure in the debate about democracy in the Islamic world. He was a leading theologian and is considered to be one of the fathers of Arab nationalism. In *The Nature of Despotism*, Kawakibi criticizes the spirit of injustice dominating the Islamic world, more precisely in the form of the Ottoman Empire, and presents new means by which to escape it, namely, the Western concepts of liberty and democracy. Kawakibi saw the European model as a best practice and argues for the adoption of this model (Nouh 2003). His book was meant to introduce the concept of a new governance ideology and to raise awareness of its utility as a means to end suffering from injustice. It should be emphasized that

4 His book was translated into French shortly after its publication, and Kheyreddine himself edited the translation. This explains his aiming to reach readers in Europe, too.

5 He insists on peace and justice as the guarantee for life.

Kawakibi does not use the term "democracy" in his book; rather, he uses a new terminology of "constitutional *democracy"* (*al-shoura al-dustouriyya*) (Al-Kawakibi 2011, 29). He employs this term in the introduction of his book without even explaining it. "Constitutional democracy" is in Arabic a combination of an Islamic term meaning "advice" and the Western concept of a constitution. Kawakibi refers to Western European countries as an example for how this system might function; this hybrid concept would rectify the injustice committed in the name of Islam by the Ottoman Empire.

Thus, both Kawakibi and his predecessor Kheyreddine saw governmental reform as the best way to general reform; they saw the establishment of democratic political and social institutions rather as a duty of rulers to their Islamic subjects. They maintained that democracy should be implemented by leadership and the apparatus of the state regardless of how the masses might consider this endeavor. In theological terms, Kawakibi argues, and likewise Kheyreddine, that the spirit of democracy can be found in Islamic Sharia, so that his contribution could be considered as an attempt at the islamization of democracy.

Summing up, Muslim thinkers of the 19th century could consider democracy only within theological Islamic framework and were unable to transgress the borders of Islamic political and social doctrine. They first became audacious enough to successfully address democracy outside the theological framework only in the aftermath of the downfall of the Ottoman Empire in 1924. The book written by Ali Abderrazek exemplifies this new tendency (Ali Abderrazek 2013, 25). It was written in 1925, when Islamic theological and political classes were still under shock after they perceived how Kemal Atatürk, the father of the new nationalist Turkish state, moved away from classical Islamic Sharia, the classical concept of Islamic Khilafat, and even substituted Arabic Letters in the Turkish language by Latin. The Kemalist Turkey regarded the method of governance and the majority of Islamic characteristics of the Ottoman Empire as a lasting heritage, they were declared useless and were substituted with Western concepts that Atatürk claimed to be more efficient and promising. Ali Abderrazek, the leading theologian and teacher in al Azhar, defended this attempt and argued that this change would help to develop the Islamic world. He added that Western democratic concepts can be used by Muslims to improve their own situation. He added that Islam doesn't have any specific system of governance that should be preserved; rather, as he stated, Islam distinguishes between political and religious affairs. Abderrazek thought it to be legitimate and religiously permitted to adopt new forms of governance as long as they do not harm the spirit of Islam. Ali Abderrazek's position was harshly criticized by al Azhar leadership. Although he was member of the teaching board, Abderrazek lost his position and became a *persona non grata* in religious institutions in Egypt and the most Muslim states of that time. His writings were like an earthquake in Muslim modern thought; they are still a subject of debate, sparking reactions and contradictions between and among Muslim scholars. Ali Abderrazek's position supports the assumption that Muslim theologians of the 19th and 20th century were not against democracy; rather, they saw it as an instrument with which to bring prosperity to the Islamic world.

Returning now to the discussion of how Muslim scholars of the 19th and first half of 20th century tried to understand democracy and to introduce it to the Islamic world, there is no evidence of the involvement of the public in this discussion. It is self-evident that Kemal Atatürk received no public support for his introduction of Western concepts. This serves as proof that democracy at that time was still an elite issue in the Islamic world. The fact that this region saw several uprisings and revolts in 19th century did not justify the need for democracy. People were clamoring for economic and social justice, but there is no evidence of a public claim to the Western concept of democracy.

When the majority of the Islamic states became annexed and dominated by European colonial powers, the idea of Western democracy faded from theological discourse. During this period, democracy became the alleged doctrine and sometimes the stated purpose of colonialism. Indeed, this term harkens back to the *mission civilisatrice*. European colonial powers presented colonialism as a way of propagation of Western values of democracy and human rights. Both Muslim elites and the masses perceived democracy and liberty to be the ideology of the enemy and to be therefore indefensible. However, this situation would dramatically change after the independence of those countries. With the emancipation of the Islamic world from colonial hegemony and the establishment of Islamic nation states, democracy appeared in a new form, namely, a more concrete one, and it became a useful political ideology in several Islamic states.

2. Muslim elites as Western-trained democrats

The first generation of politicians and intellectuals who took power in the Islamic states after independence was mostly trained in the West. They were fascinated by the Western way of life; they adopted it and tried to push the masses to accept it as well. This is the period in which Islamic nation states embraced the ideology of democracy. As a case in point, the majority of the political regimes in the Islamic world of that time endorsed democracy, and the terms "democratic" and "republic" played a prominent role in the naming of those states.[6] It should be stressed that it was also in this period that democracy was advocated by the elite. Yet there were no public reactions in form of strikes or uprisings, nor public claims to democratic rights. Thus, democracy was rather something for the elite, not for the public. This can be explained by the fact that Islamic societies were still suffering from high illiteracy rates and social underdevelopment, to the point that democracy lay beyond the expectations of the masses.[7] In the period from 1980 onward the situation went in a fundamentally different way: the Islamic world would see waves of revolts demanding democracy. The case of the Iranian revolution of 1979 may be interpreted as the first step in this process; the Arab Spring would be interpreted as the most recent development in this regard.

3. The shift of democracy from the elite to the public

The Iranian revolution of 1978/79 was a mass revolt against a dictatorship that, on the one hand, promised Western concepts of modernism and governance but, on the other hand, was positioned against any kind of freedom of opinion or liberty. Theologians supported this revolution; they belonged to the same class of intellectuals who organized and supported leftists and unions. During the revolution and shortly thereafter, both the masses and the Iranian elite laid claim to the same values of liberty and freedom. Shortly after the successful revolution, the Iranian governing regime, which was gaining power and vanquishing its enemies, chose another ideology that rejected the Western concept of democracy and substituted it with *wilayat al faqih*, which again denotes an elite incarnation of democracy unexpected by the public (Moussawi 2011, 39).

---

6 There was also a strong socialist nationalist movement in this period, which endorsed the concept of democracy, specifying it as a socialist democracy in contrast to a liberal (Western) idea of democracy.

7 The Muslim world is still suffering from illiteracy, which was very strong in previous decades. According to specialists of this region, this is one of the main handicaps of development and progress in these countries.

Regardless of the further developments in Iran and the fact that the Iranian state defines itself as Islamic rather than democratic[8], the Iranian revolution of 1978/79 was the first public movement calling for democracy in the Islamic world in that period of time.[9] It encompassed a shift in the perception of democracy. Until that time, the discussion in the Islamic world was dominated by regimes and elites who claimed to be democratic and accused the masses of not being ready for democracy. The Iranian revolution demonstrates how brutally the elite regimes reacted to the public demand for democracy and justice.

This revolution transformed into an authoritarian religious regime that persecuted opposing parties and free voices in Iran. This fact shows that democracy can become dangerous for the established regimes in the Islamic world when it is taken up as a public rallying cry. This was also the case in Algeria in 1990–92 (Volpi 2003, 37). In both the Iranian and Algerian cases, theologians and religious parties were among the main actors and architects of the uprisings whose main slogan was that of implementing democracy. Notwithstanding, theologians in Iran became a vicious opponent of democracy after they won the coup against the dictatorship. Muslim and religious parties in Algeria, however, ended up in jail, and they still didn't abandon their claim for more democracy and justice. What happened in these two countries was the prologue to the reforms that took place in many other countries, which arguably culminated in the Arab Spring of 2011.

Putting aside the question of whether the Arab spring was a conspiracy, the events of the years 2010–11 involved millions of people in Tunisia, Morocco, Libya, Algeria, Egypt, Jordan, Syria, Sudan, including men and women, workers and unemployed people from different classes, ethnic and religious groups, all of whom took to the streets to demand democracy. This was the moment in which democracy became distinctly public in the Islamic world. It also explains the brutality of the regimes enacted against those uprisings. The echo of this public movement reached all other countries in the Arabic and Islamic world, and it evoked a strong fear that democratization would dismantle every regime in the region.

Returning now to the question of theology, the Arab spring was neither a religious movement nor a religious revolution; religious movements

8 This new dichotomy Islamic versus democratic is still understudied.

9 There was another uprising in Sudan in 1964 which didn't have the same strength or power.

were not the main catalyst behind it. Nevertheless, religious parties in many Arab countries were among the first paradigms that paved the way for those revolutions; religious revolutionaries were the first victims of those despotic and autocratic regimes as they were also against dictatorship. During the Arab Spring, democracy, human rights, and transparency were fought for by everyone regardless of his or her religious affiliation.

4. Democracy and Muslim life in the West

"Islam and democracy" is perhaps one of the popular conference titles in the last decade in Western countries. This subject has attracted people because it usually deals with the alleged opposition between Islam, democracy, human rights, and secularity. Added to these assumptions is the complicated discussion about Sharia in Western secular societies. To support the supposed contradiction of Islamic faith to Western values, people usually present either the hyper-conservative Muslim groups (Salafist groups) living in Europe or the behavior of some Islamic regimes such as Saudi Arabia, Sudan or Afghanistan as an example for what they think to be the "real face" of Islam. These examples demonstrate the deteriorating situation people face there but do not give clear answers to the questions articulated in this paper.

To understand the matter of "Islam and democracy" in a Western context, it is useful to exchange the paradigm of research from Islam to Muslims. This means that, instead of asking about the general classical theoretical Islamic position regarding democracy, it is far more relevant to examine how Muslims living in Western countries define themselves and perceive democracy and Western values. To illustrate this, I will take the Muslim community in Germany as a case study. There are four main groups of Muslims that may be considered for this purpose. The first consists of ultraconservatives – Salafi Muslim groups, who are usually cast as being a danger to society and who themselves claim to be the only and legitimate representatives of the Islamic faith.[10] This group does not represent more than one percent of the total Muslim population in Germany (Bundesamt für Verfassungsschutz 2017). In this matter, terrorists and

10 The field research done by the Ministry of the Interior in Germany in 2007 gives important details about this issue; see Brettfeld/Wetzels (eds.) (2007), 464.

Salafists should be distinguished from one another. In Germany the majority of Salafists are political Salafists, not terrorists, while the people who are qualified as terrorists in Germany almost always have a Salafist background (ibid.). Like most radical groups, German Salafist groups do not believe in most values of Western societies; not only Western people but also the majority of their fellow Muslims are regarded as bad Muslims or even as apostates (kāfir). The ideological position of this group is rather negative; they reject the modern concept of political participation and call for the re-establishment of what they deem to be an authentic classical Islamic regime (ibid.). Due to their small number, they cannot be taken as representatives of Islamic theology.

The second group is that of the official Islamic organizations, which mostly have a religious background; however, in the last years few Islamic secular organizations have been established. Although several secular Muslim organizations have unanimously stated their belief in democracy, some organizations have not. The study conducted by the Ministry of the Interior in 2007 stated that some of these organizations still maintain an unclear position vis-à-vis the values of democracy and human rights. Nevertheless, they have been found to incite their members to be active in democratic organizations (Molthagen 2002). Moreover, they vocally affirm their recognition of democratic secular law, i.e. German law.

Muslim intellectuals and religious personalities make up the third group. They are grouped together because they bridge the gap between the mainstream Muslims and the German government. This group has two subgroups: on the one hand, there are active theologians such as imams; on the other, there are theologians employed by universities and intellectuals. The Graz Declaration of 2003 clarifies the opinion of European imams (Khalfaoui 2015, 304–340). This document expresses the submission of imams to democratic secular law, the recognition of democracy, and the rejection of all forms of violence. The same position is to be found in the opinion of the German Organization for Islamic-theologian Studies (DEGITS), founded in 2015 by members of theology studies departments in Germany (including students and teachers alike). This young organization recognizes also democratic institutions.[11]

The last group can be considered to be mainstream Muslims. This is the general Muslim population, and a substantial percentage has become

---

11 See the German Organization of Theological Studies (DIGITS), http://www.migazin.de/2015/07/15/islamische-theologen-gruenden-fachverband/.

German citizens. This group has no concrete opinion against democracy or secular law, and their main interest is securing a stable life for themselves and their families. Due to the cultural and political background of the most migrants in Germany, there exists no credible threat to democracy from Muslims. The majority of Muslim comes from Turkey, former Yugoslavia, North Africa and, most recently, from Syria. All of these regions and states have an established secular tradition, and there exist no societal ills like polygamy or religious marriages. The fear of parallel justice enacted among and by Muslims has been also summarily rejected by recent research (Rohe 2017). Thus, the majority of German Muslims and European Muslims do not present any threat to democracy and can even be considered as enriching to democracy. They regard democracy as an opportunity and want to benefit from it. The new Muslim generations are actively working on new projects, trying to develop their communities, and the trend is only growing.

References

Al Kawakibi, Abd Ar-Rahman (2011): *Tabāʾiʿ al Istibdād wa maṣāriʿ al Istiʿbād,* Cairo: Kalimat Arabiyya.

Al Tounsi, Kheyreddine (rep. 2012): *Aqwam Al Masālik fi maʿrifat ahwāl al mamālik*, Beirut: Dar al Kitāb Al lubnāni.

Ali Abderrazek (2013): *Islam and the Foundations of Political Power*, Edinburgh: Edinburgh University Press, Agha Khan University.

Brettfeld Katrin, Wetzels, Peter (eds.) (2007): *Muslime leben in Deutschland, Integration, Integrationsbarrieren, Religion und Einstellung zu Demokratie*, Berlin: Bundesministerium des Innern.

Bundesamt für Verfassungsschutz (2017): Salafistische Bestrebungen, https://www.verfassungsschutz.de/print/de/arbeitsfelder/af-islamismus-und-islamistischer-terrorismus/was-ist-islamismus/salafistische-bestrebungen (accessed 8.4.17).

Khalfaoui, Mouez (2015): Das islamische Recht und das staatliche Recht aus muslimischer Perspektive, in: Rohe, Mathias (ed.), *Christentum und Islam in Deutschland. Grundlagen, Erfahrungen und Perspektiven des Zusammenlebens*, Freiburg: Herder, 304–340.

Lewicka, Magdalena (2014): Between the East and the West Aqwam al-masālik fī ma'rifat ahwāl al-mamālik Khayr ad-Dīn at-Tūnusī (1822–1890), *Planeta Literatur. Journal of Global Literary Studies*, No. 1, 2014, 53–68.

Molthagen, Michael (2002): Die "Islamische Charta" des Zentralrates der Muslime in Deutschland (ZMD), http://zentralrat.de/3035.php (accessed Mar. 4th, 2017).

Moussawi, Ibrahim (2011): *Shi'ism and the Democratisation Process in Iran. With Focus on Wilayat al-Faqih*, London: Saqi Books.

Nouh, A. (2003): Al-Kawakibi: sawt al Nahda al 'Asrawi, in: *Center of Studies of Union Arab, Qira'at fi al fikr al Arabi*, 89–105.

Qureshi, M. Naeem. (1999): *Pan-Islam in British Indian Politics: A Study of the Khilafat Movement, 1918–1924*, Leiden: Brill.

Rohe, Mathias (2017): Mathias Rohe, Mahmoud Jaraba, *Paralleljustiz. Eine Studie im Auftrag des Landes Berlin*, Berlin: Senatsverwaltung für Justiz und Verbraucherschutz.

Sharabi, Hisham (1970): *Arab Intellectuals and the West: The Formative Years, 1875–1914*, Baltimore: Johns Hopkins Press.

Tarabischi, George (2000): *Min al-Nahda ila al-Ridda*, Beirut: Dar Saqi.

Volpi, Frederic (2003): *Islam and Democracy: The Failure of Dialogue in Algeria*, London: Pluto Press. 2003.

How does the Christian Faith Enter Politics – and What Does it Do There?

"Faith-based politics" after the Separation between Politics and Religion

Matthias Möhring-Hesse

The separation between politics and religion, like its institutional substrate, the separation of Church(es) and State, is a constitutive foundation for democratic societies. This is a conviction that democrats, but also theories of democratic societies, regard as self-evident. "Faith-based politics", i.e., political activities that the actors in question carry out as an expression and aspect of their faith, therefore stands under the basic suspicion of undermining the separation of politics and religion, thereby violating a precondition of democratic societies and being "fundamentalist", at least in the sense that, for the political sphere, religion advocates untenable and even destructive religious truths. Seen in this way, not only certain forms, but every form of politically engaged religion creates problems for democratic societies, even if such societies may be robust enough to "endure" at least the softer variants of this problem and only "suffer" from its hard variants.

By theologically reconstructing "faith-based politics" and by reconceptualizing the separation between politics and religion that is constitutive of democratic societies, this paper aims to reject this *fundamental* suspicion of *every* "faith-based politics" – with the explicit knowledge that political debates in democratic societies are indeed burdened by fundamentalist religions and the religious truths they advocate with a claim to absolute truth. First, the separation between politics and religion is grasped as the result of a symbolically mediated practice of boundary-drawing carried out "from the inside", in order to avoid a substantialist understanding of both politics and religion (1). On this foundation, "faith-based politics" is theologically shown to be the practice by which the faithful person masters the situational challenges of his or her faith through political engagement, i.e., by "doing" politics to confirm and actualize himself or herself in it as a faithful person (2). Considering that politics is essentially a public event and thus consists primarily of public communications, two essential pragmatic goals are reconstructed from "faith-based politics" and its secular realization (3). The faithful can realize these two goals only to the degree that their religious convictions and attitudes have a prior secular meaning and are religiously meaningful convictions and attitudes only on this basis (4).

1. The Separation between Politics and Religion

In ancient Greece, with the term "politics", the idea of the political was also "invented", the idea namely that citizens of a community deal with their communal interests and thereby also with the order of their community together, though conflictually (Meier 1995). The citizens of the Greek city-states did not separate politics from religion, whereby they had no concept of this religion and while religious matters, as understood today, probably were not all that important in their politics. Politics arose from and consisted in the citizens' engaging in it together – and permitting other citizens, though not women, children, or slaves, to engage in their communal political activity. As a concept, "religion" arose in another context; namely, in the Roman Empire, it meant the conscientious fulfillment of ritual duties – and was thereby an integral component of the Roman social and legal order (Wlosok 1970). After Christianity was raised to the state religion of the Roman Empire, the claim was derived from Christianity that it was the sole true religion. But only in early modern times did Christianity, including in its self-description, become a religion (Feil 1986). At the same time it was denied, from out of the Christian religion, that Christianity was a religion and thus merely "a work of man". At the time of their "discovery", at any rate, the two forms of practice, politics and religion, did not stand opposite each other and were not separated, and each probably "possessed" aspects of the other form of practice that was discovered elsewhere.

That these two forms of practice have moved apart is usually presented in the separation of Christian Church and State, often using the term "secularization". Ernst-Wolfgang Böckenförde's pertinent and often noted essay was not the first to reconstruct the "Entstehung des Staates" (rise of the state) as a "Vorgang der Säkularisation" (process of secularization, Böckenförde 1991). But the idea that the profane state is the end result of a long-lasting process of secularization does not correspond very well with the events and developments discussed in the essay (Dreier 2001, 6ff.) – and specifically not with those in Germany, either: the emerging nation-state that is neutral toward religion (or denominations and Churches) was based for a very long time on the system in which the ruler picked the State Church, a fusion of state rule and religious or Church leadership that was especially intense by historical comparison. The image of a religion that wrests itself free of the state and that had to withdraw from the matters integral to the state is not very plausible, considering that the matters that we, at least today, grasp under the terms "religion" and "Church" only emerged in the separation of Church and State – and thus religion or Church and State are simultaneous achievements of historical development.

Even if we can thus doubt that the concept of secularization is a good key to understanding the separation of Church and State, we will not therefore deny this development, at least not for the countries shaped by Christianity. Won in France against the Roman Catholic Church, enforced in the United States of America with and for the religious communities, and developed in Germany out of confessional splits and struggles, over the centuries at the latest, in these countries states developed that monopolize sovereignty and thereby make and can enforce societal decisions – and at the end of this development are not only under the rule of law, but are also democratically constituted (cf. Cavuldak 2015). To this end, state rule – and the medium of implementing rule, the law – were "profaned", i.e., "freed" of religious matters both in their language and in their legitimation; at the same time, the states made themselves neutral toward religions, religious communities, and Churches respectively present in them. The legitimation and orientation of state rule were stripped from the particular religions and confessions; additionally, the states placed themselves at a distance from the communities and Churches representing these religions and confessions, suppressed at least their direct influence, and instead submitted them to the states' law and the rule mediated by that law.

Not least through that, religions became a part of the societies ruled by states. With their particular symbolic systems and cognitive specificities, with the convictions and attitudes mediated in them and their systematized doctrines, and with their particular forms of practice, denominationally fragmented Christianity and with it also other religions have "withdrawn" to become a particular part of society – and thereby *became* religions. At least in its dominant form, the Christian religion – especially in Germany – was represented and shaped by the Christian Churches. In the various countries shaped by Christianity, various relations of delimitation and cooperation emerged between the state, on the one hand, and the Church(es), on the other. In distinction especially from the *laïcité* typical of France, for Germany since the Weimar constitution, we speak of a "lagging separation" – seeking to grasp with this substantively and semantically unsuitable term the religion-friendly policy of the German state, which awards to the Churches and, because these, also to other, if only a few other religious and ideological communities a high degree of self-administration and state privileges, above all the legal status of statutory bodies under public law.

The separation between religion or Churches and State, however, does not (yet) show that politics and religion simultaneously stepped apart as two different spheres. In order for states to develop on a democratic foundation, first the ancient idea of politics, which had been buried for centuries, had to be taken up again. Though this form of practice did not tally with the nation-states of the various countries, it nonetheless had its essential focus in the state. For only in the state do modern societies have an adequately efficacious instrument with which communal interests and the order of the respective social relations can be enforced. Since politics is therefore related to the state (though not exclusively) and because in politics an increasing plurality of interests and forms of life, but also of the "ultimate truths", the powerful convictions and values, must be mastered and at the same time the claims of deliberative rationality must be served, this particular form of practice was profaned through the mutual expectations of the actors driving it – and the "ultimate truths" were thereby driven out of it in such a way that such "ultimate truths" cannot drive politics, at least not successfully. Thus, while the air became thin for "ultimate truths" in contexts of political practice, they find outstanding conditions in the sphere of religion; and religious communities and especially by the Christian Churches took them up, organized them, dogmatized them, and – finally – demanded them from the faithful. By setting mutual boundaries that they, together, can regard as meaningful, actors separated them step-by-step and, over a long period, grasped them as two different spheres of their symbolically mediated practice or – to use the terminology of Pierre Bourdieu – as two different social fields (Bourdieu/Wacquant 1996). Because they are socialized under the conditions of this separation, actors are shaped by the attributions of meaning embedded in politics and religion, by what they perceive, and by how they interpret these. By implementing these meanings in their practice, they make use of and reproduce the boundary-drawing between politics and religion. Actors know when they engage in politics and when they implement their religiosity – and know how to operate competently, and that means differently, in the two fields of politics and religion.

This separation between politics and religion thereby remains below the level of differentiation that is usually addressed in theories of differentiation. Both politics and religion have their own symbolic systems, their own doctrines, and definitely their specific forms of practice. The two symbolic systems are not so alien to each other that they can't be connected, mediated, and mutually translated. On the contrary, the language of politics flows into the field of religion, as one can see in the central concepts precisely of Christian theology, for example the concept of justice. But vice versa, as well, actors in the sphere of politics cannot do without religious symbols – and this not only when (for example with the term "cult of personality") they want to problematize dislocations in this sphere. For example, the term "Creation" has a fixed position in environmental debates, even though it obviously cannot be used without alluding to God as the Creator. Despite their separation, politics and religion are permeable to each other.

2. "Faith-based politics"

Ernst Michel (1689-1964) used the term "faith-based politics" (German: "Politik aus dem Glauben") to designate political engagement that the actors in question understand as an expression of their Christian faith – in such a way that their Christian faith is "preserved" (Michel 1926, 20) in these politics. Conceptually, he distanced this engagement from a Catholically organized politics – and thereby opened the theological access to political practice of faith through the forms of expression that it had found in German social Catholicism. In the following, when the focus is on the presence of the faithful in politics and on theologically reconstructing this presence under the conditions of the separation of politics and religion, Michel's term will be taken up gladly. The Christian religion in particular has a necessarily communitarian dimension, and precisely this communitarian dimension is implemented in the form of practice that is captured in "religion" and the sphere delimited as religion. Nonetheless, this approach would inappropriately focus theological attention on "only one" of various forms of political practice that are intentionally tied to the Christian faith. So, in the coming theological reconstruction, it is important to take as broad an approach as possible, and that means working from the faith of the actors who embody the religion and precisely not from the sphere of religion that they jointly "populate". That is what the term "faith-based politics" will stand for in the following.

Adherents have both the cognitive and the habitual aspects of faith, i.e., specific convictions, certainties, attitudes, and stances (this is the pragmatic premise of the following considerations) as an aspect of their action. These aspects do not lie outside of their action – and therefore are also not to be understood as something temporally or causally preceding their action. The matters designated by the noun "faith" thus exist only as aspects of the action designated by the verb "be faithful". If this verb refers to a specific action, one will ascribe it to actors who understand themselves as the faithful – and that means who understand themselves as being in a relationship to God and who, through this self-understanding, determine who they "are", including in front of others. Based on this self-understanding, these actors will interpret their action as faith, and others will interpret their action in the same way because of a known or announced self-understanding. To the degree that the faithful usually don't "invent" their God, but "find Him" in the traditions of Christianity and appropriate ideas about and attitudes toward God that are transmitted in those traditions, they understand themselves not only in relation to this God, but also – even if not unbrokenly – in relation to Christianity, for whose traditions they "can thank" God.

Understanding oneself in relation to God has a holistic aspect, at least if one has gotten to know this God in Christian contexts. The faithful accordingly know themselves to be "entirely" and "always" addressed by this God, even if they do not (and cannot) remain aware of this "entirely" and "always" either always or as an "entire" person. The holism of the relationship to God typical of Christianity, however, is not transposed to the action that the faithful term "faith". That God always and entirely addresses them does not mean that they are faithful always and in all their actions – including when they always and unceasingly act as accountable actors.

With the aid of the "quasi-dialogical" model of action suggested by Dietrich Böhler (Böhler 1977), the action termed "faith" can be extracted from the stream of the faithful's action and specified more precisely: actions are characterized not only through observable operations and the goals attributed to them, but also through the situations in which the operations are observed and interpreted as situations for the attributed goals. Both in self-interpretation and in interpretation by others, the relationship between situation and actors is thereby two-sided: action situations *are relevant to* actors, whereby it is the actors who perceive, from the perspective of possible action, which of the circumstances and events surrounding them are relevant to them and in this sense "select" the occasions of their action. On the other hand, individuals *act* in situations and thereby react to these situations or to certain aspects of situations that are relevant to them. Colloquially, we say that one "ends up in" a situation, that it "happens" to or "befalls" us, and that we are "confronted" with it. We thereby express that the situation is something that precedes our action (or inaction), but that challenges us because it "concerns", "interests", or "is relevant to" us (Böhler 1985, 252). In their action, actors "answer" situations that they first interpret as "questions" and that, in precisely this way, they have constituted as situations of their action. Only by interpreting external conditions or events as "questions" are they provoked to give practical "answers". "If that is correct, then it may be asserted that both the possible genesis and the necessary function of an action, namely to alter, shape, or master situations, has a quasi-dialogical structure" (ibid. 257).

Based on this theory of action, it is possible to gain a specific understanding of the faithful's actions described as "faith": their action situation can make actors see themselves as challenged in their relationship to God and thus in their self-understanding as faithful. Based on their self-understanding, they interpret experiences of their action situations as a "question". Their action can be termed faith if they seek to "answer" such "questions" in such a way that in these action situations they live up to to their relationship to God and thus realize themselves as faithful. Faith is thus the "answer" to such action situations, which the faithful interpret as inquiries into their self-understanding as faithful. This concept of faith does not address every action of the faithful as faith, because although the faithful are always the faithful, they are not always challenged in precisely this self-understanding and consequently need not always confirm themselves as the faithful in their action. Only such action is addressed as "faith" through which the faithful seek to master action situations that challenge them as the faithful and therein in their relationship to God – and seek to master them in such a way as to confirm their relationship to God and through it themselves as faithful (cf. Möhring-Hesse 1997, 83-206).

Because faith is tied to a corresponding interpretation of action situations, others cannot simply interpret the action of the faithful as faith on the basis of a known self-understanding. It is not possible to see from the outside whether their action is faith, i.e., a practical implementation of their relationship to God. Others may have good reasons to arrive at corresponding interpretations of the situation and then to interpret the action of the faithful as faith. But ultimately, they depend on receiving corresponding information from the faithful themselves that their action situations address their relationship to God as challenges – and that they themselves interpret their action as faith and thereby make it identifiable for others.

In what religion concretely is for the faithful, they find an outstanding site where they are challenged as the faithful in such a way that they must confirm themselves in their relationship to God and thus as the faithful. It is downright paradigmatic that, in religious services, the faithful urge each other to profess their faith and at the same time "accept" this profession. But this site does not completely encompass their faith, which is in principle possible in all sites of differentiated societies and also outside of religion. In principle, the faithful can be challenged everywhere in their relationship to God and thus as faithful ones, so that in this situation they must confirm themselves as the faithful and only in this way thereby master the challenge of precisely these situations – and this even when they are unable to put this challenge into words for the respective others and therefore cannot communicate it (Möhring-Hesse 2008; on this, cf. Telser 2013 and Kreutzer 2016).

Contexts of political practice can become this kind of situations, and political engagement can become a form for mastering the challenges resulting from them. Then the faithful carry out their political engagement as the faithful – and carry out "faith-based politics". They exert influence on the shaping of their social circumstances and "negotiate" these circumstances with others – precisely therein confirming themselves in their relationship to God and realizing themselves as those who have faith in this God and who live in hope of Him. As much as this engagement is politics, it is equally also faith. This faith is in principle partial, to the degree that not all situations of the political engagement of the faithful (must) become challenges to their faith and to the degree that their politics need not always "serve" the implementation of their faith. Politics then serves to secure interests "beyond" the identity as faithful, though even then it is possible that, on a deeper level of self-interpretation or more fundamental attitudes, this political engagement, too, is understood as an expression of their own faith and is correspondingly intended. If "faith-based politics" is theologically reconstrued in this way, this does not affect the noted separation between politics and religion, to the degree that "faith-based politics" is political engagement in the social field of politics and faith is therefor "outside" the field of religion, even if is not independent of this field.

At least if one imagines the God hoped for in Christianity as one present in human history and pressing for human salvation and if one cannot imagine this God except as the salvation intended for all people, one will suspect that political contexts not only *can* become challenges for the faithful and that politics not only *can* serve to master these challenges. Rather, one will assume that, for the faithful, politics is very probably a matter of faith: those of the faithful who understand themselves not only as addressees, but also as independent subjects of a salvation for all humankind that God brings into human history, will ineluctably "come" into situations in which they must engage in politics in order to realize themselves as the faithful in their relationship to the God who is beneficial for all people. In this sense, Edward Schillebeeckx is not the only one who rightly speaks of a "political dimension of the Christian faith in God" (Schillebeeckx 1987, 92).[1]

3. *The Pragmatics of Public Faith: Convictions and Becoming Understandable*

After politics and religion separated into two different spheres of symbolically mediated forms of practice, "faith-based politics" is situated in a special way, namely "placed" in a sphere of politics separated from religion. In this sphere, actors expect each other to engage in politics, i.e., to seek to shape their common social circumstances and to use power to that end, thereby mustering at least a certain orientation toward the common welfare, willingness to compromise, and other things; but they do *not* expect from each other that they intentionally tie their political engagement to their faith, and they do *not* expect that one of them engages in politics in order to thereby confirm himself or herself in his or her relationship to God and as a faithful person. Unlike the sphere of religion, the actors in the sphere of politics do not have joint access to the attitudes and convictions needed to give such a connection between faith and politics meaning; nor do they have a common language to create such a meaning. If the sphere of politics becomes the situation of Christian faith, then the faithful see themselves called upon there to master the challenges of the situation and to engage in politics to this end, but that means to fulfill the expectations and counter-expectations that constitute this sphere. "Faith-based

1 When Schillebeecksx and other theologians speak with great generality of the "political dimension" of the Christian faith and identify politics not only as a highly probable, but beyond that as a necessary form of carrying out Christian faith, then this results from his concept of politics, which is as comprehensive as conceivable: politics as the "intense form of societal engagement [...], an engagement possible to everyone" (Schillebeeckx 1987, 99).

politics" is not excluded from the sphere of politics because of the separation between politics and religion; but this sphere with all its particularities becomes the precondition for "faith-based politics" and limits the possibilities to successfully confirm and realize oneself as one of the faithful through politics.

First, "faith-based politics" can be successful only if the faithful "find" ends and means with which they can master the problems and dislocations that they experience as challenges to their faith. If they see themselves challenged as the faithful by, for example, discrimination, hostilities, or curtailments by people in the narrower or broader surroundings, for example because of the "option for the poor" inherent in their faith, and if they arrive at the conviction that the only suitable way to answer this challenge is to change their social circumstances, then they must "find" the politics with which they can strive for this change; and they must also explore the respective political field and establish themselves as political actors in this field – in the best case, together with others who have the same or similar convictions. In the political engagement thus "found", they master the situational challenge and thereby *successfully* confirm themselves as the faithful – and this, whether or not their engagement is also politically successful and they are able to enforce the projected changes together with others and against yet again others. However, the change intended with "faith-based politics" depends on precisely this political success, for which reason this success, too, lies in the intention of "faith-based politics". With the exception of situations of extreme injustice, in which political resistance can become a question of one's own authenticity, political success also lies in the intention of "faith-based politics" – and, along with the successful confirmation of the faithful as the faithful, it is thereby their second, as if outward-directed criterion of success.

Since its invention in Greek Antiquity, politics has been a decisive communicative enterprise: one engages in politics through the public "exchange" of opinions and their justifications. In this way, political actors persuade others; they collectivize their interest situations and their representation or they come to compromise agreements with others and thus bring themselves into accord. One way or another, they gain power and thereby increase their chance to prevail with their own interests over others. All attempts to generalize particular interests through general rights and thereby to identify intended changes as just are dependent on public communication. The faithful (too) will successfully engage only to the degree that they are successful in the communicative processes that constitute politics. Two types of communication intentions can be distinguished that pragmatically determine "faith-based politics".

If the intention of the faithful is to realize themselves as the independent subject of the salvation irrupting into human history from God, for example by redressing discrimination, limitations, and dislocations and by arranging their social circumstances differently, then they must convince the respective other actors in the respective political field that the projected changes are in the general interest of all and in this sense are just or that they lie in the common interest at least in some sense. The precondition for their being able to convince this or that other person is that they are understood with their expressions and justifications of their political opinions. The others must therefore be able to deduce the meanings of the expressed opinions and reasons, i.e., they must also, for example, know what interests they have, if the claimed generality or at least the claimed commonality of interests is true. Only on the basis of such understanding is it possible for others to be convinced by reasons, to agree through insight to the politically pursued changes, and, convinced in this way, to engage in politics in the same direction. And only on the basis of mutual understanding is it conceivable that political actors spur each other on with opinions and reasons and "negotiate" a common politics. Consequently, "faith-based politics" is pragmatic only when and to the degree that it can, first, make itself, its intended changes, and their justification understandable for other actors in the political field in order to be able then to convince the respective others.

The requirement to make themselves understandable already makes it necessary, in political communication, for believers to use a language that abstains from the particularities of their faith and to transcend attitudes and convictions that can be plausible only in the context of their faith. To the degree that they thus cannot use the language that, after the separation between religion and politics, is "given" only in the sphere of religion, and to the degree that they must transcend precisely those convictions and attitudes that "have" meanings at least there, the faithful engage in the secular communication that constitutes the sphere of politics.

A second intention typical of the faithful in the public communication they conduct in the sphere of politics is less ambitious: they can want to make their "faith-based politics" so understandable that other political actors understand why these politics are an expression of their faith and thereby "essential to faith". Here, their intention is not to convince others of their politics. Rather, others are to be familiarized with the intentionality of their political engagement and with the "seriousness" and "urgency" inherent in it. To this end, they must not only make it understandable to their addressees what changes they seek to have prevail and for what reasons; beyond that, they must make it understandable that, with these politics, they are answering matters that challenge them in their faith and that with these politics they seek to master these challenges and precisely thereby to confirm themselves in their faith. They do not need to speak completely and comprehensively about their faith, but they do need to speak enough about it that others can understand what it means to believe something and to be challenged in this faith by the respectively discussed matters in the world that are "outside" of the religion – and this, even if the others do not share this faith and cannot even understand why believers "have" this faith. The faithful will not be able to do this entirely without borrowing from the language of their faith and entirely without referring to the convictions and attitudes that are part of their faith. But they must put all of this into a secular language understandable to those who do not know this language of faith and who do not share these attitudes and convictions – and who are able, from what they can also understand, to fill with meanings the "islands" of what they don't understand. A prominent example of this kind of communication is the social encyclical "Laudato si´" (2015), in which Pope Francis not only makes the case for an ecological-social transformation and offers a secular environmental ethics, but at the same time also wants to make known a religious, unsecularizable ethics of Creation and spirituality from which the faithful view the lasting concern about the shared planet Earth as a matter of their faith and consequently "take" corresponding engagement as the practice of their faith.

To make oneself understandable in these two ways is not a precondition for being permitted to engage in secular discourse in the field of politics, as it was treated, starting with John Rawls and Robert Audi, in the Anglo-American debate about the secular justification of religious citizens (on this, cf. Schmidt 2001). It is simply a pragmatic condition of their participation in political discourses and the communicative representation of their "faith-based politics". To make oneself understandable is an imposed "constraint" only in that it is the precondition for successfully taking part in public negotiating processes in the sphere of politics. To make oneself understandable in the public representation of "faith-based politics", however, is also a question of competence, as Jürgen Habermas discussed in his essay "Religion in the Public Sphere". If they propound their "faith-based politics" in the sphere of politics, believers must be able to make themselves understandable with their opinions and reasons and additionally to "step outside" the language specialized for their faith but available only in the sphere of religion. Habermas' implication that religious actors do not start out with this competence and that secular citizens are more skillful at least in public justification is rather improbable in the federal German context. The common and in this sense secular language in which political citizens can make themselves understood is namely not predefined by the separation between politics and religion. It does not result until there are processes of public negotiation in which actors not only "exchange" their opinions and reasons, but must also jointly "find" the language in which this exchange succeeds. That unreligious and in this sense secular citizens can be presumed to have it easier in this cannot be recognized, especially since they face similar "identitarian" and thus similarly structured challenges as religious citizens do to make themselves understandable with their politics. In addition, not only the unreligious, but also religious actors have carried out and still carry out the separation between politics and religion through symbolically mediated practice, so that this separation and consequently also the "rules of the game" of politics are as familiar (or unfamiliar) to the one group as to the other. Because the faithful are socialized politically and religiously under the same conditions of the separation between politics and religion, one should assume that believers can propound also their "faith-based politics" competently, and that means in a generally understandable way and in this sense secularly.

4. The Priority of Secular over Religious Meaning

Matters that the faithful experience "beyond" their religion as challenges to their faith are shaped by their historical context, and, precisely in this shaping, become challenges to the faithful that they "must" master through the particular form of practice of politics. What the faithful experience as challenges is thus already previously charged with meanings and becomes challenges to their faith with precisely these prior meanings – and beyond that, becomes religiously significant. In this case, too, what Edward Schillebeeckx (1914-2009) identified as fundamental for religious meaning and thereby also for revelation holds true: namely, that every "religious meaning of a worldly process [...] presupposes a human meaning" (Schillebeeckx 1990, 29). If historical matters, for example discrimination of, hostilities toward, or the limitations placed on people, are interpreted as challenges to one's own faith, then these matters are attributed a religious meaning and they are "asserted" to be relevant for the relationship between God and the people He considers with benevolence. This religious interpretation of historical matters presupposes that these were previously interpreted as important matters "without direct relationship to God – 'etsi Deus non daretur'" (ibid.) – and in this sense as secular. Without prior secular meaning, however, the asserted religious meaning of the practice of "faith-based politics", namely the challenge to faith and the mastery of this challenge through political engagement, is invalid; but then "faith-based politics" is senseless secularly as well as religiously.

Historical matters prove to be secularly important under the conditions of their respective context of meaning – and thereby, in political questions in public communication, in the sphere of politics. That people are discriminated against, are subjected to hostility, and are curtailed in relation to others, that they are denied comparable rights and full inclusion in their social contexts, and that this is injustice against them – this and other things emerge if the corresponding assertions and their justifications can hold up in public communications. In political contexts, therefore, the "human meaning" (which is the precondition for religious meaning) emerges in public communication, or fails there. Thus, the picture usually drawn is veritably reversed: only in political debates do secular meanings develop which then become a challenge to the faith of believers and in this sense can become religiously meaningful. Because matters in the sphere of politics become ("are made") meaningful, they can also become meaningful for believers, also in a special way for their faith, i.e. religiously meaningful. So religion is not the first thing, which is then laboriously translated into the second, politics; rather, politics is the first thing that, for believers, becomes a problem in their faith and thereby religiously meaningful. Thus, "faith-based politics" does not initially format itself politically in religion, but in politics – and thus in precisely the opposite way from how it is drawn in the aforementioned debate about the secular justification of religious citizens, as well as by Habermas in his reconstruction of the public presence of the religious.

For the faithful, the priority of secular over religious meaning need neither always, nor necessarily manifest itself in a corresponding temporal sequence. Temporally, believers can thus definitely experience politically relevant matters as challenges for their faith and then "choose" political engagement to master them – and only "tread" the sphere of politics through this engagement and "participate" in the meaning jointly found there. But in these cases, as well, they must reproduce the priority of secular meaning – and, in the sphere of politics, they must ensure that the challenges to their faith and that the "faith-based politics" chosen to master these challenges have corresponding secular meanings. To put a fine point on it: believers ensure the justice of "faith-based politics" in political discourses, i.e., in the sphere of politics and not in the sphere of religion – and this justice is the precondition that enables their politics to be valid as the practice of their faith and thereby as "faith-based politics", also in the sphere of religion and in relation to their brothers and sisters in faith in the religious language available to them in common.

Social-ethical literature often finds it interesting (as does Habermas, as well, in his essay "Religion in the Public Sphere") that, via the political engagement of the faithful, religious orientations inspiringly enter politics, open new perspectives or alternatives to well-trodden paths there, or enable previously blocked agreements. Orientations that are available only in religious language and that are interwoven with the attitudes and convictions characteristic of religions flow, via "faith-based politics", into politics – and have beneficial effects there. This "direction of flow" of meanings need not be excluded because of the priority of secular over religious meaning. Even if the religious meaning of politically relevant matters cannot be had without their secular meaning, these two different attributions of meaning will have mutual influence, so that not only will secular meaning shape religious meaning, but also vice versa: religious meaning will shape secular meaning. But even if, through "faith-based politics", religious orientations exert influence on the meanings discovered in politics of politically relevant matters, their religious meaning is decided by their ability to flow into the politically found meanings – and thereby in this context their ability to "gain" a secular meaning. But regarding this as a process of secularization does not grasp it well: if religious orientations gain a secular meaning, they are precisely not subsumed in this secular meaning. On the contrary: in relation to the secular meaning discovered in politics, there is a "surplus" of meaning in "faith-based politics" that the politically significant matters "have" for believers in their relationship to God.

References

Böckenförde, Ernst Wolfgang (1991): Die Entstehung des Staates als Vorgang der Säkularisation [1967], in: Ernst W. Böckenförde, *Recht, Staat, Freiheit. Studien zur Rechtsphilosophie, Staatstheorie und Verfassungsgeschichte*, Frankfurt am Main: Suhrkamp, 92–114.

Böhler, Dietrich (1977): Zu einer philosophischen Rekonstruktion der "Handlung", in: Günther Patzig et al. (eds.), *Logik, Ethik, Theorie der Geisteswissenschaften.* XI. Deutscher Kongress für Philosophie, Göttingen, Hamburg: Meiner, 306–317.

Böhler, Dietrich (1985): *Rekonstruktive Pragmatik. Von der Bewusstseinsphilosophie zur Kommunikationsreflexion*, Frankfurt am Main: Suhrkamp.

Bourdieu, Pierre; Wacquant, Loïc (1996): Die Logik der Felder, in: Pierre Bourdieu, Loïc Wacquant, *Reflexive Anthropologie*, Frankfurt am Main: Suhrkamp, 124–152.

Cavuldak, Ahmet (2015): *Gemeinwohl und Seelenheil. Die Legitimität der Trennung von Religion und Politik in der Demokratie*, Bielefeld: transcript.

Dreier, Horst (2001): Kanonistik und Konfessionalisierung – Marksteine auf dem Weg zum Staat, in: Georg Siebeck (ed.), *Artibus ingenuis. Beiträge zu Theologie, Philosophie, Jurisprudenz und Ökonomik*, Tübingen 2001, p. 133–169 (also in: JZ 2002, p. 1–13, available online: http://www.jura.uni-wuerzburg.de/fileadmin/02160100/Elektronische_Texte/JZ_2002_1–13.pdf.

Feil, Ernst (1986): Religio, Vol 1: Die Geschichte eines neuzeitlichen Grundbegriffs vom Frühchristentum bis zur Reformation, *Forschungen zur Kirchen- und Dogmengeschichte* 36, Göttingen: Vandenhoeck & Ruprecht.

Habermas, Jürgen (2005): Religion in der Öffentlichkeit. Kognitive Voraussetzungen für den "öffentlichen Vernunftgebrauch religiöser und säkularer Bürger", in: Jürgen Habermas, *Zwischen Naturalismus und Religion. Philosophische Aufsätze*, Frankfurt am Main: Suhrkamp, 119–154.

Kreutzer, Ansgar (2016): Authentisches Zeugnis. Zwischen theologischer Affinität und soziologischer Skepsis, in: Ansgar Kreutzer, Christoph Niemand (eds.), Authentizität. Modewort, Leitbild, Konzept. Theologische und humanwissenschaftliche Erkundungen zu einer schillernden Kategorie, *Schriften der Katholischen Privat-Universität* 1, Regensburg: Pustet, 279–306.

Meier, Christian (1995): *Die Entstehung des Politischen bei den Griechen*, 3rd ed., Frankfurt am Main: Suhrkamp.

Michel, Ernst (1926): Politik aus dem Glauben, in: Ernst Meier, *Politik aus dem Glauben*, Jena: Eugen Diedrichs, 7–27.

Möhring-Hesse, Matthias (1997): Theozentrik, Sittlichkeit und Moralität christlicher Glaubenspraxis. Theologische Rekonstruktionen, *Studien zur theologischen Ethik,* Vol. 75, Freiburg/Schw. [et al.]: Universitätsverlag [et al.].

Möhring-Hesse, Matthias (2008): "Überall" glauben in ausdifferenzierten Gesellschaften. Eine soziologische Verortung christlicher Glaubenspraxis in theologischer Absicht, *Ethik und Gesellschaft*, 1/2008, available online: http://www.ethik-und-gesellschaft.de/pdf-aufsaetze/EuG-1-2008_Moehring-Hesse.pdf.

Schillebeeckx, Edward (1987): *Weil Politik nicht alles ist. Von Gott reden in einer gefährdeten Welt*, Freiburg im Breisgau: Herder.

Schmidt, Thomas M. (2001): Glaubensüberzeugungen und säkulare Gründe. Zur Legitimität religiöser Argumente in einer pluralistischen Gesellschaft, *Zeitschrift für Evangelische Ethik*, No. 4, 248–261.

Telser, Andreas (2013): Differenzierung und Interpenetration von Religion und Politik – theologisch, in: Ansgar Kreutzer, Franz Gruber (eds.), Im Dialog. Systematische Theologie und Religionssoziologie, *Quaestiones disputatae,* 258, Freiburg et al.: Herder, 356–380.

Wlosok, Antonie (1970): Römischer Religions- und Gottesbegriff in heidnischer und christlicher Zeit, *Antike und Abendland,* 16, 39–53.

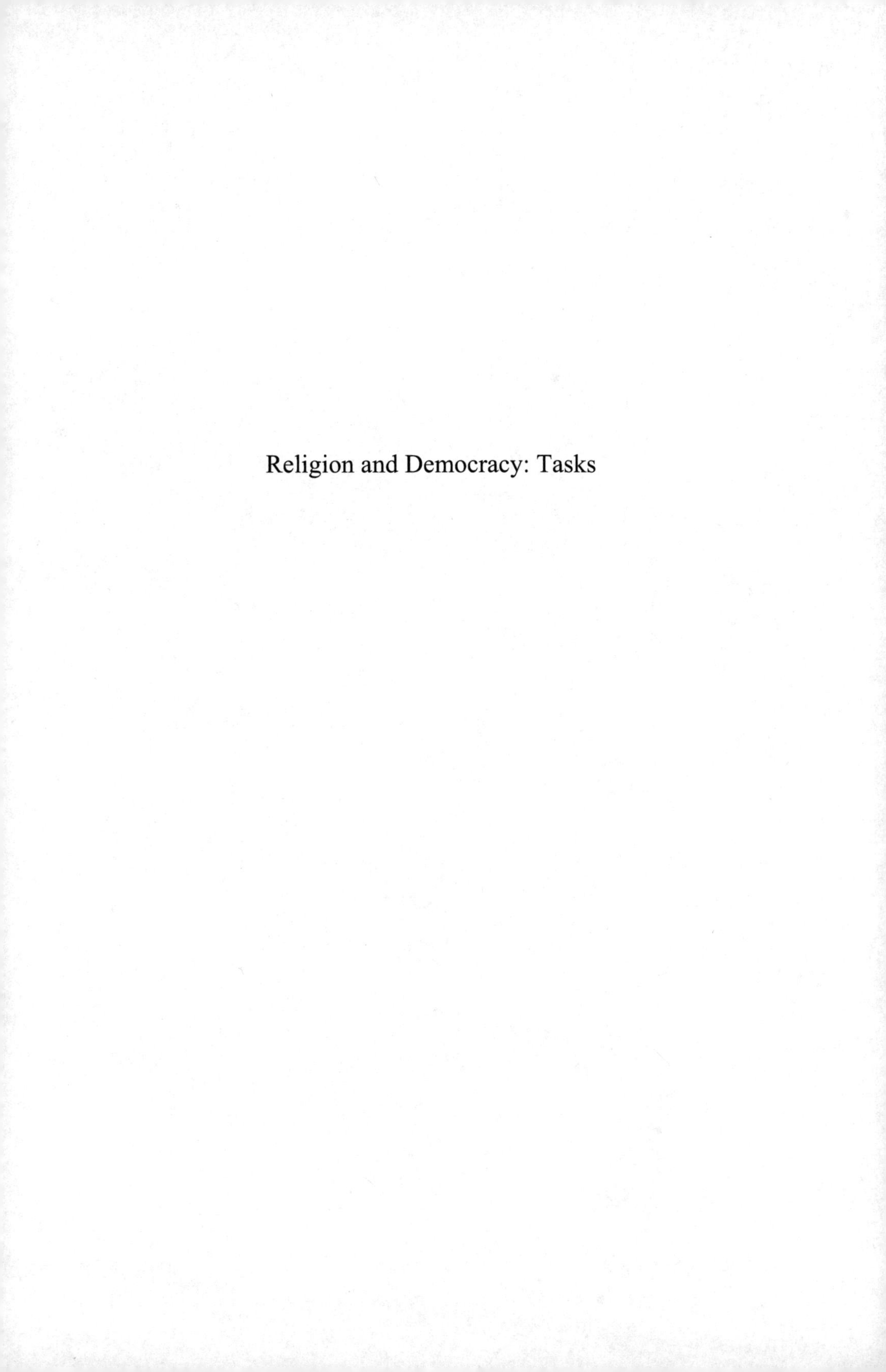

Religion and Democracy: Tasks

Who Is Responsible for What I Do on Facebook to Democracy?
A Public-theological Reflection on the "Responsibility" of Media-users for Democratic Culture

Florian Höhne

Introduction

Every year the US-American magazine "Time" names a "person of the year". The list of "the most influential persons"[1] includes people as diverse as John F. Kennedy, Joseph Stalin, Bill Clinton, Elizabeth II, Martin Luther King Jr. and Pope John Paul II.[2] Then, in 2006 the person of the year was: "you" – because of the internet and the contribution of all those communicating in the World Wide Web. Lev Grossman (2006) wrote, "And for seizing the reins of the global media, for founding and framing the new digital democracy, for working for nothing and beating the pros at their own game, TIME's Person of the Year for 2006 is you."

In his book on "Internet and Democracy", Stephan Eisel (2011, 272) refers to this decision of TIME-magazine in order to illustrate the importance of what every individual does in and through the internet – and Eisel does so under the headline "individual responsibility". While also emphasizing the important role of "political decisions", big companies and the state, Eisel (2011, 274f.) claims, "Liberal democracy relies on the responsibility of individuals, but she cannot […] solely rely on this."

Both do something similar, the TIME-Magazine implicitly and Stephan Eisel rather explicitly: they both impute responsibility for the development of democracy also to the individual participant in media-communication. Of course, such an imputation is not absurd in the horizon of democracy, participation rights and emancipation. Media such as newspapers, TV pro-

---

1 Cf. http://www.zeit.de/politik/ausland/2015-12/bundeskanzlerin-angela-merkel-time-person-of-the-year, my translation. If not indicated otherwise, the translation of German quotes has been done by the author of this paper.

2 Cf. http://content.time.com/time/specials/packages/completelist/0,29569,2019712,00.html.

grams, blogs or social internet-platforms are of political relevance because they mediate political discourses and constitute publics in which public opinion is (trans)formed and injustice should be criticized.[3] They would not have this relevance without the people who watch TV, read newspapers or blogs or provide content for the internet-platforms – be it on old-school-homepages or in the social web. This makes it coherent to see all these people as "co-responsible" (see below) for the media-culture and its function for democracy.[4]

Such an imputation is not new in the debate on media ethics – at least in the German speaking context (Filipović 2010) – and it gains importance in the internet and the web 2.0 (Jansen 2003, 312; Filipović 2010). Especially in the web 2.0 the distinction between producer and user does not convince anymore, because consumers are producers of content as well (Filipović 2010; Costanza & Ernst 2012, 9) – in Facebook, Youtube or Wikipedia, for example, they are "prosumers" (Costanza & Ernst 2012, 9). This makes the question of the responsibility of consumers – or prosumers – even more pressing.

Such responsibility-talk seems to meet basic orientations of Public Theology. As I have argued elsewhere Public Theology is oriented to foster the possibilities to participate in society and discourse, especially the possibilities of those least privileged. A theology of the cross can make this reasonable (Höhne 2015, 97f.). On the first glance, "responsibility" seems to highlight such active participation. In a similar sense, the term "responsible society" has been used by the ecumenical movement (Strohm 2000, 205).

The responsibility of media-users or "prosumers" could be reflected in a multitude of perspectives.[5] While these are all relevant, I will focus on the term "responsibility" in this paper. The reason for that is the prominent role the term plays in media ethics, where it has been called a key category (Funiok 2011, 68; Veith 2002, 381), and in theological ethics as well as in public debates: in the latter, it is often used as "responsibility-rhetoric" (Günther 2002, 120) or an appeal without clear meaning or consequence

---

3 For some of these and other functions of the public cf. the short overview in Jarren & Donges (2006, 98). Cf. also Debatin (1998, 120).

4 Similarly, Heidbrink & Schmidt (2011) have emphasized that it is not only producers who bear responsibility in the economic system but also consumers.

5 For example, it could be reflected from the standpoint of empirical research in how communication works or what effects it has on discourse culture and politics, from communicational theory, sociology or theory of democracy.

(Debatin 1998, 113, 116; Funiok 2011, 63). In the last time, "responsibility", and especially its attribution praxis, has been criticized sociologically and philosophically. This makes one question the emancipative role of "responsibility". On this background, my question is: How can Public Theology talk about the moral[6] responsibility of media users and "prosumers" (in accordance with its orientation to participation)? To put it more concretely: How much am I responsible for what I do on Facebook to democracy? My intention in dealing with these issues is not to deconstruct the concept of media users' responsibility but, on the contrary, to make it more effective.

Approaching the topic, I will first exemplify how the media-user's responsibility can be conceptualized. Secondly, I will summarize important motives of the critique of "responsibility" in order to get a deeper understanding of the ambivalence of responsibility and its imputation. Acknowledging these critiques, the paper closes with the suggestion for how to use "responsibility" in media ethics.

1. Responsible publics: "ethics for media users"[7]

How can we conceptualize "responsibility", and especially the "responsibility" of media users, in terms of media ethics? This question suggests itself not only because "responsibility" is a "key category" to media ethics (Funiok 2011, 63, 65, 68; Veith 2002, 381) but especially because it is the key concept in ethical focus on media users. In 1989, Clifford G. Christians (1989) asked for the responsibility of the public; not later than 1996, Rüdiger Funiok and Wolfgang Wunden followed, conceptualizing media user ethics as a reflection of the (share of) responsibility of the recipients (Funiok 1996, 107) as citizens, participants in media communication and educators (Wunden 1996, 125); Veith (2002, 381) introduces responsibility as "main idea", and Gregor M. Jansen (2003) works with the tension of freedom and responsibility.[8]

6 For the difference between moral and legal responsibility see for example Debatin (1998, 117). The focus in this paper is on moral responsibility.

7 For this translation of "Publikumsethik" see the title of the article quoted by Debatin (1998, 128, footnote 37).

8 For a list of publication on ethics for media users that includes the named works see Filipović (2010).

To answer the question, I will mainly display Rüdiger Funiok's account because it develops a concept of moral (cf. Funiok 2011, 63) responsibility and places the user ethics in the framework of a more general media ethics that integrates the responsibilities of producers, enterprises and politics (Funiok 2011, 14–17, 155, 159). To clarify and enlarge certain points I will draw on other theories.

Funiok introduces "responsibility" as a "key category" into his media ethics because "responsibility" qualifies the way to come to concrete ethical judgements (Funiok 2011, 64f.). Thereby, he wants to take the term from Max Weber rather than from Hans Jonas (ibid., 64). Responsibility is for him the headline for "considering consequences of actions" in ethical reasoning (64 [my translation]).

Funiok develops a more concrete understanding of responsibility with reference to Bayertz' "'classical' concept of responsibility" (65), which he expands with Bayertz himself, Hubig and Rophol (65–69). According to this concept, responsibility basically means the imputation of action effects to an acting subject, which presupposes a subject with at least some degree of will, freedom and foresight (65). Especially the attribution of a minimal degree of freedom to act, which implies having at least two options for what to do or not to do, is named as "precondition for attributing responsibility"[9] by Stapf (2006, 149f.), Debatin (1998, 115f.) and Funiok (2011, 65). This presupposition can be summarized as "agency".[10] In addition to this, responsibility presupposes according to the classical concept an evaluative system that qualifies the action effects as harmful, and an instance that one has to be answerable to and – as I may add – that thereby holds one accountable for these (65f.). While Funiok elaborates further on that,[11] these basic elements of responsibility may suffice here: someone

---

9 Stapf (2006, 149–151) has discussed this precondition together with two others (causality and foreseeability) thoroughly.

10 Funiok does not explicitly say that his understanding of responsibility presupposes (organized) "agency" of the one responsible. But he makes a certain degree of «autonomy of action" ("Handlungsautonomie") and having alternatives a presupposition for being held responsible (Funiok 2011, 65).

11 In these elements, Funiok (2011) makes this more concrete with Hubig and adds with Rophol the temporal dimension and the modus of action (68); thus, the analysis of the term "responsibility" leads to the following matrix with seven elements, articulated in my terms (68): a Subject (A) is accountable for an (undone) action's (B) consequences (C), which is evaluated by certain norms (D), answering to an instance (E), at a certain point in time (before, after or during the action)(F), in a certain way (G).

(1.1) is – retrospectively or prospectively (68) – responsible for something (1.2) in front of an instance (1.3).

1.1 Responsibility of the public …

The basic idea of "Publikumsethik" is, of course, to make the public responsible or, more precisely, "co-responsible"[12]. Funiok (1996, 108–112) has made this plausible by an "anthropology of the public" in which the public's activity is emphasized: members of the public consciously choose what they watch and read, and even watching and reading in themselves are active insofar as they include interpretation and evaluation; media contents are discussed (1996, 109f.). The more recent development in the World Wide Web towards a "prosumer" (see above) adds another kind of activity to this list and makes the image of the active user even more evident.

Locating the public in the subject position of the one (co)responsible makes the ambivalence of the TIME-magazin's person of the year 2006 poignant: Is the "you" second person singular or plural? Whom exactly does the "you" refer to? With reference to Lenk und Maring's (1995, 249f., footnote 2) understanding of "collective action",[13] one can distinguish three possible answers: individuals are individually responsible, a coordinated collective has "corporative responsibility", and a non-coordinated collective might have a "communal responsibility" (Christians 1989, 258).

In the framework of Debatin's (1998, 118f.) and Funiok's (2011, 70–72) concept of responsibility, the imputation of responsibility to two entities is plausible, to individuals or to corporations, because only these two meet the conditions Funiok (65) made for being responsible: agency, freedom and foresight[14] – corporations of cause in a more complex and indirect way (Debatin 1998, 119; Stapf 2006, 152). While individual responsibility is close to an average understanding of responsibility (cf. Heidbrink

---

12 Funiok (1996, 107, 112, 155) uses the German term "Mitverantwortung".

13 Lenk and Maring (1995, 249) introduce "collective action" (and "collective responsibility") as generic terms for uncoordinated and coordinated action.

14 For criteria like this and the discussion about the possibility of corporative responsibility see the summary in Stapf (2006, 152–158). Stapf (2006, 153f.) sees the possibility of extending responsibility to corporations because they fulfill the preconditions for being a responsible subject.

2003, 38, 46), the matter is more complex for corporations, especially as soon as one understands these – as Funiok does – as more than just the addition of individual elements (Funiok 2011, 70). According to Funiok (2011, 70f.), corporations can and need to be held accountable for corporative actions, plans and decisions because corporations define ends (based on values), possess "organizational means" and plan strategically. Corporations can be responsible – as Stapf (2006, 153f.) argues with reference to Peter French – because they are capable of acting, of making decisions in an organized way. Based on this, it is reasonable to talk not only about individual responsibilities that add up to a sum but also, and clearly distinguished[15] thereof, about corporative responsibility. This allows to debate the relation of individual and corporate responsibility to each other – as Funiok does (70f., 73; Lenk & Maring 1995, 250f.).

Clifford Christians (1989, 257f.) has explicitly introduced the "communal responsibility" of the public as a third form alongside with the "task responsible" and "corporate responsibility". At some point in his argumentation Funiok (2011, 69, 157) also named the society or the public as being responsible (but he omits these in another chart; cf. ibid., 72). Does it make sense to impute responsibility not only to individuals and organized collectives but additionally to the public as such? This is at least problematic because the public lacks being organized – as Funiok (2011, 157; 1996, 115) himself points to – and it lacks (addressable) agency (Neidhardt 1994, 13f.).[16] With pretty much this argument, Bayertz (1995, 55) criticizes the idea of responsibility of humanity as such while allowing corporate responsibility.

In order to hold the "public as a collective" (Funiok 2011, 157) responsible, one would either have to develop a concept of responsibility that works without organized agency[17] or to create an organizational form for the public as such.[18] Christians (1989, 258f.) motivates his concept of col-

15 For the difference see for example Lenk and Maring (1995, 273f.).

16 "Insgesamt erfüllt das Publikum nicht die Organisationsbedingungen eines kollektiven Akteurs. Seine Handlungsfähigkeit stellt sich in der Regel über die Summe von individuellen Reaktionen her, die nur auf unterster Ebene konzertiert erscheinen." (Neidhardt 1994, 14)

17 For a discussion of the issues occurring if one attributes responsibility for "non-corporative collective action", see Lenk and Maring (1995, 252–257).

18 For a similar argument see Heidbrink (2003, 46): "Die Übertragung von Verantwortlichkeiten auf höherstufige Handlungssubjekte konfligiert mit den Prämissen, daß nur natürliche Personen über Eigenschaften verfügen, die sich zu Verantwortungsträgern machen. Hierzu zählen Gründe, Motive, Intentionen

lective or communal responsibility with the intuition that public sentiments are powerful, the (silent) public approval of nuclear armament, for example. While this intuition is probably true and – if so – definitely establishes his thesis that society is not beyond moral issues (259), it still gives no account for holding or making the public as an uncoordinated collective responsible as an agent.[19] At least in this article, Christians is obviously not interested in addressing the attribution problem but rather in establishing a universal duty to sustain culture.[20] If the intention of establishing "communal responsibility" is to emphasize everybody's responsibility and to give an incentive to establish, for example, organized groups for media control, this intention can be appreciated – but imputing responsibility to an unorganized collective might turn out to counter this very intention: where everybody is in a non-specified way[21] responsible for nearly everything, no one needs to feel occasioned to effectively take this re-

---

und Interessen, aber auch Wahlfreiheit, Kenntnisse und Einflußmöglichkeiten. Sollen Korporationen oder Kollektiven diese Eigenschaften zugschrieben werden, bedarf es entsprechender Modifikationen – oder neuer Kriterien, durch die Verantwortungsfähigkeit auf impersonaler Ebene definierbar wird. [...] Handlungsfähigkeit muss unterstellt werden können, damit Handlungsfolgen zuschreibbar sind." While the latter – to presume the capacity to act or be an agent – is still plausible for coordinated collectives, this does not apply for unorganized entities like the public.

19 Bayertz (1995, 55) uses a similar argument in a different context: "Die Tatsache, daß alle diese individuellen Handlungen sich zu einem Gesamtresultat addieren und oder multiplizieren, konstituiert noch kein distinktes Subjekt, dem dieses Resultat zugeschrieben werden könnte."

20 Christians (1989, 258) nearly explicitly says so: "Zudem führt die Behauptung, wir trügen beispielsweise für Technologie wie Großcomputer, Satelliten, Nuklearwaffen und Raumfähren kollektive Verantwortung, zu sehr komplizierten Problemen, wenn man die Frage der Urheberschaft klären will. Und kann man die Schuld für zugefügten Schaden und irgendwelche Pannen im Wirkungsfeld der Massenmedien [...] überhaupt noch sinnvoll jemandem direkt zuweisen? Trotz derartiger Einwände behaupte ich, daß sich eine große Anzahl von Menschen gleichzeitig eine und dieselbe allgemeine und undifferenzierte Verantwortung teilen kann." Such neglect of the question of how to attribute consequences is in this context possible because Christians (ibid.) nearly nullifies the difference between "responsibility" and "duty".

21 Christians (1989, 259) himself points to this lack of specification: "Das Konzept der kollektiven Verantwortung hindert uns mit anderen Worten – obwohl es nicht in der Lage ist, bestimmten Personen einen genauen Anteil an konkreter Verantwortung nachzuweisen – an der falschen Schlussfolgerung, daß Gesellschaften Größen ohne Moral seien." For the problem see also Debatin (1998, 121).

sponsibility.[22] This is as problematic as overloading the individual with responsibility it cannot take (Debatin 1998, 119), which happens if an individual really feels occasioned to individually take this "collective" responsibility.[23] Thus, communal responsibility of the public can be plausibly understood only as a necessary highlighting of the responsibility of every individual media users[24] and of a corporation of media users and not of the public as collective. Plausibly, it can be about everybody's responsibility.

Hence, "Publikumsethik" is in Funiok's framework about the responsibility of all individual media users as social beings and of somehow organized groups of users which he names, for example, "Media-Watch-Dogs-Initiative[s]" (Funiok 2011, 157). His user ethics is linked to his demand for a (self)education towards "media-competence", which takes care for the conditions for responsible media use (ibid., 155, 172f.; 1996, 119f.).

1.2 …for the functioning of democracy…

What are people responsible for? Still more generally, Funiok (2011, 74, in similar words) has answered this question with the distinction of three basic responsibilities: for oneself, for the social environment, for the natural environment. More concretely, he names explicitly (among other responsibilities) the co-responsibility of the media users as citizens for the political culture (158, 169): "Als *Bürger und Bürgerinnen* tragen wir eine

---

22 For a similar problem see also Heidbrink (2003, 47) on the "Dilutionseffekt geteilter Verantwortlichkeiten in höherstufigen Prozessen", Debatin (1998, 119), Funiok (2011, 67) on "Verantwortungsabwehr oder –abschiebung", Funiok (2011, 163) and Lenk and Maring (1995, 241, 265). Bayertz (1995, 67) describes this problem in a different context: "Wo alle verantwortlich sind, kann prinzipiell kein Unterschied mehr zwischen denen gemacht werden, die verantwortlich sind[,] und denen, die es nicht sind. Und damit verliert die Rede von Verantwortung tatsächlich jeden deutlichen Sinn."

23 For the inadequateness of both extremes see also Lenk and Maring (1995, 246f., 282).

24 Similarly and in coherence with her own criteria, Stapf (2006, 184) understands the public's responsibility as the media user's individual responsibility. Nevertheless she also lists the collective responsibility of the public (187, picture 13). Funiok (1996, 108) relates "Publikumsethik" also primarily to individuals.

soziale Mitverantwortung für das Funktionieren demokratischer Institutionen und damit auch der Medienordnung" (158).

Thinking Funiok's approach further,[25] a more specific classification of political functions of publics in democracies can help to make this responsibility more specific. Neidhardt (1994, 8f.[26]) distinguishes three "principals and functions": (A) "The public shall be open to all social groups and all topics" in order to fulfill its function to create transparency; (B) topics shall be dealt with "discursivity" in order to fulfill the validation-function; (C) thereby, public opinions shall emerge publically so that the public has an orientation function (Neidhardt, 1994, 8f.).

People in the public take co-responsibility for all three functions (A, B, C) insofar as they are engaged in media politics, media legislation and supervision of public broadcasting stations (Funiok, 2011, 158f.). In their individual media use they support the first function (A) insofar as they use media to keep themselves up to date politically, avoid being deceived by manipulative or wrong information (158f.) and publish truthful and nuanced information. They participate in the public discourse (B) insofar as they write letters to newspapers (158), collaborate in local TV-projects (158) and produce content in the internet in a manner appropriate to discourse. They act responsible in the third sense (C) by forming and transforming their own opinion by media use independently (158).

1.3 …in front of an instance

In front of what does one have to be answerable for one's actions (done as well as left undone)? Closely linked to this is the question who socially holds responsible and who attributes responsibility – a question that becomes more important as soon as one refrains from basing responsibility in ontology, as if one were responsibly by the "nature of things"[27] (Funiok

25 Funiok (2011, 15) himself connects the task of media ethics with the "ideal functions of media".

26 For this see also Jarren and Donges (2006, 98).

27 Bayertz (1995, 20f.) puts it similarly in German: "Verantwortlich 'sind' wir nicht durch die Natur der Sache, sondern werden wir in bestimmten sozialen Kontexten 'gemacht'. Angemessener als ein objektivierendes oder ontologisierendes Verständnis ist es daher, Verantwortung als Ergebnis einer *sozialen Konstruktion* zu deuten, d. h. als eine spezifische Deutung eines sozialen Problems und den Versuch seiner Lösung."

2011, 66 quoting Bayertz 1995, 4, 20f.). The question is of special importance for an internet ethics because here attribution is particularly difficult. Greis (2001, 232f.) names the following reasons: in internet communication, the agent often could not know whether his utterance was read or had any effect, and she or he could often take the utterance back anytime. And – from the other side – the author might not be retraceable (Funiok 2011, 184).

While not being more specific in the part on user ethics, Funiok (2011) generally names two instances that attribute responsibility ethically: social attribution (66) and attribution by the subject itself (67), stressing the necessity of the latter for any talk of responsibility "in the proper sense" (67). If responsibility is ethically always a question of the subject's commitment, the named attribution problems will be solved insofar as they are relocated in the subject. But it leads to a new problem: "defense against responsibility" (67), which Funiok (2011, 68) wants to solve through an "institutionalization" that can only work "as long as individuals and corporations involved really take their share of responsibility and commit themselves." This, however, is obviously not a solution but a reformulation of the problem. Another solution he names is media education: the willingness to take responsibility, especially to take responsibility for what one publishes in the internet, would be part of media competence (173). Still, attribution is finally left to the subject itself. One element of the first instance (social attribution) is a subject he does not name explicitly but performs: the ethicist himself attributes responsibility. Every written or outspoken ethics for media users is a more or less specific attribution of responsibility to the media users.

1.5 Sum

Ethics for media users emphasizes the responsibility of every media user, prosumer and their organized associations, including the political responsibility for the functioning of democracy. The call for media education can be understood as a call for establishing the condition for this kind of responsibility. If the "responsibility" works as Funiok displays it, it would emphasize the participation of recipients in media communication and in the democratic process.

2 The problem of responsibility

So far, the imputation and taking of responsibility have been treated as something unambiguously good. In the more recent debate, the ambivalences of "responsibility" have been discussed. I summarize three critical points, which Vogelmann's (2014, 33–40) work pointed me to, and apply them to web communication.

2.1 The problem of diffusion

Ludger Heidbrink (2003, 27, 45) expounds the tensions and consequences of a "diffusion of the principal 'responsibility'"[28], which rests on the "expansion of areas of human knowledge and action" and which would overwhelm the term. His analysis is based on his sociological description of modern societies as highly complex societies, which are on the one hand functionally differentiated in a multitude of systems with semantics specific to each system and on the other hand coined by the overlapping of those functional areas (27f., 39f.). In this complexity, "responsibility" has become the "leading paradigm for issues of legitimacy" (35) because it could be stretched to meet the needs of decision-making and regulation problems in complex societies without secure knowledge (19, 35, 43f.): the term has been stretched, so that one can be made responsible for consequences in the far future (35f.), for the mass of unforeseeable emerging consequences that appear in complex processes (36), and so that one could also take responsibility as a company or nation and not only as a person (37) (cf. also Vogelmann 2014, 34).

On the one hand, "responsibility" is needed: Heidbrink does not argue in favor of abolishing all those "expansions" of responsibility (49, 307).[29] Rather he suggests limiting such expansions by putting them under the condition of being well-founded by usefulness (306f.). Such limitations were necessary because – on the other hand – the stretching partly overstretches[30] the concept of responsibility, as the problems in the term and

28 Cf. Vogelmann (2014, 33), see there also for a brief summary of Heidbrink's thesis. For this "diffusion" see also Lenk and Maring (1995, 241) and Funiok (2011, 67).

29 Heidbrink (2003, 19) emphasizes the capacity of the concept "responsibility".

30 Vogelmann (2014, 34) uses a similar term in German. Heidbrink (2003, 48) uses the term "Verantwortungsüberdehnung".

its tensions show (45). Most of them appear to me to be tension between the expanded use of responsibility in complex situations and the traditional (37) or common-sense understanding of the term.[31] Used as such, the principal responsibility "exceeds the limits of what could be rationally attributed to someone, includes areas and events that – from a rational standpoint – lay beyond what could be integrated into a theory of action" (19). Such an expansion of the use of responsibility would, according to Heidbrink, empty the concept (19). But to lose a potentially helpful concept is not the only threat. Another one is obvious where Heidbrink summarizes the "problematic ambivalence of the term" as follows: "We need him [the term responsibility, FH] to include side effects of our actions into the present horizon of moral reasoning. Simultaneously, the term in his normal (and normative) use seduces to overestimate the knowledge of intractable structures and the possibilities to interfere." (48)

On this background, media ethics will have to be careful about to whom precisely it attributes which responsibility. Heidbrink's criticism intensifies the problem of attributing responsibility to an unorganized collective because it makes it possible to see this attribution as part of an overall development in which the term "responsibility" is not only stretched but overstretched. Having Heidbrink's (2003, 306f.) own suggestions in mind, it seems reasonable to rather stick with the limited responsibility of individual media users and of cooperatives. In addition to this, however, an ethics dealing with web communication also can learn from Heidbrink not to yield to the temptation of responsibility talk to overestimate the steering power of individual entities in complex dynamic processes.

2.2 The problem of discipline and capability

Klaus Günther (2002) has focused on another aspect of the "inflationary use of the term 'responsibility'" (118). Often such use was ignorant of the conditions for imputing responsibility (118; Vogelmann 2014, 37). Having discussed the complexities of imputation practices in law or ethics, he

31 These are, for example, the tension between the expansion to consequences in the far future and the common-sense limitation to a more limited time span (Heidbrink 2003, 45), between the imputation of responsibility for the outcome systemic processes and "global consequence" on the one hand and the linear causality of the traditional term (45) or between imputation to collective actors and traditional imputation to natural persons (46).

mentions some basic contextual conditions for prospective as well as retrospective (125f.) imputation: the subject's "capacity to act" (126), the consequence's foreseeability and controllability (126) and the subject's internal and external conditions including material and social resources (127). This makes a complex understanding of the "capability to act"[32] the condition for a "just attribution" (128) of responsibility.

In connection with this, Günther explains the "ambivalent experience" of finding oneself in the position to be self-responsible (120f.). On the one hand, this can empower the subject that is liberated from external control to recover "own forces and abilities" (120). On the other hand, being made responsible can be experienced as being disciplined (122). The latter will be the case inasmuch as the subject understands its own responsibility differently and/or lacks the capability this responsibility requires (121, 128f.): "It is expected of them to understand themselves as a person they are not, cannot become or don't want to become." (129)

Hence, responsibility talk becomes problematic where it leaves out of sight the actual or potential capability of those whom it attributes responsibility to. Taking this into account, the media ethicist can only speak of the responsibility of media users insofar as she makes sure the users are capable thereof. Rüdiger Funiok (2011, 155, 172–174) does so by demanding media education and media competence. Where this is left out, responsibility talk is prone to have disciplinary effects at odds with an orientation to participation.

Things get more complicated when it comes to "prosumers" in web-2.0 context who do not only "consume" but also produce content. On the one hand, they obviously have the technical resources and means to produce content. This makes it possible to attribute responsibility to them for the content they produce independent of further media education. On the other hand, the plausibility of such an attribution is limited insofar as two preconditions for the attributing and taking of responsibility are not necessarily fulfilled: foresight (1) and freedom (2) (see above, Funiok 2011, 65).

(1) Alexander Filipović has described the present society as "post-redactional society": other than in John Hartley's vision of a "redactional society", people could not reflect the "consequences of their public communication" (Franzke 2016). If one cannot foresee or reflect consequences – because one is not a professional journalist and because of the dynamics of the web – while the concept of responsibility presupposes foresight

32 The word "capability" is used without reference to the capability discourse.

(ibid.), the possibility to attribute responsibility to prosumers is limited. This makes Filipović call for an education towards a "redactional society" (ibid.).

(2) Numerous writers have already pointed to the subtle manipulation of web users. Thomas R. Köhler (2012), for example, has summarized different ways how the human user is "programmed" – from "nudging" (Thaler & Sunstein, cf. Köhler 2012, 89) to "gamification" (142–157). Eli Pariser (2012) has coined the term "filter bubble": he describes how Facebook, Google and others use what they know about their users to personalize the posts and products the individual users get to see (cf. e.g. 16f.). This creates an individual informational universe for everybody – the "filter bubble" (17) which shapes our thinking (91–115). The filter itself is unchosen und invisible to the user (18f., 68) but determines the "informational diet" of each user (22). This strips one of the possibility to consciously choose a filter, to know about the blank spaces in one's knowledge (114), and thereby withdraws the possibility to decide freely (24). By limiting options of action in this way, the "filter bubble" also erodes a precondition for responsibility. Insofar this description holds true, responsibility will have to be attributed more to the authors of algorithms than to individual users in "filter bubbles".

2.3 The problem of responsibility as such

Frieder Vogelmann's own Foucault-based critique of "responsibility" is fundamental because he understands "responsibility" not only as a term conceptualized and used differently in different contexts but – more fundamentally – as an "discursive operator" that changes power relations, possibilities of knowledge and subjectifications, and that constitutes the unity across different uses of "responsibility" (Vogelmann 2014, 20f., 124f.). His formal heuristic then sketches "responsibility" as a relation of at least two positions: one imputes responsibility, one takes it (24, 125f.). The existence of these two is the necessary condition for the use of the term "responsibility" (125f.).

Vogelmann's analysis of the changing role of "responsibility" in the changing practices "labor", "criminality" and "philosophy" leads to the diagnosis of two opposing tendencies (430). On the one hand, "'responsibility' and capacity to act" become dissociated (24f., 430). Vogelmann (2014, 24, 129, 149, 159, 162, 169f., 180f.) analyzes an "*asymmetric decoupling* of the two subject positions" and an "*intensification of the self-*

relations" in the field of "labor" for instance: during the transformation of labor and unemployment, responsibility has been imputed to employees and unemployed people, which made them understand themselves as responsible entrepreneurs (140, 150, 169), thus necessitating their "self-regulation" (Honneth 2014, 12). Thereby, their self-relation is intensified because they do not simply follow imperatives but create their imperatives for themselves (157) – they actively deal with their being submitted and submitting (266) – and because they can now experience themselves as empowered and sovereign (161). Simultaneously, the position of the one responsible itself is increasingly powerless in relation to the position of the attributor of responsibility (129, 149, 162). The position to impute responsibility is the powerful one (129, 146), and its holder is not the same person as the one taking responsibility anymore (Honneth 2014, 12f.): the employees "are increasingly only 'holders' of responsibility [...] without the slightest license to held other persons or groups responsible" (13). "Responsibility" and power are dissociated (Vogelmann 2014, 162, 181, 426). On the other hand, "philosophy" has tied "'responsibility' and capacity to act" closer and closer together (24f., 426f.). Being blind for the use and effects of "responsibility" outside philosophy (427), it thereby dignifies "responsibility" even more (430, 433).

Vogelmann has entitled his book "Im Bann der Verantwortung", "In captivity to responsibility", a captivity that makes philosophy oversee its own "theoretical violence" (19, 423). This captivity becomes fatal when, as Vogelmann argues, even the philosophical critique of "responsibility" does not strike but rather stabilizes what it criticizes (433f.): even used as a philosophical ideal meant to criticize effects of responsibility, the term is used as part of a praxis determined by the "discursive operator" in which it enforces the operator (433f.) because the responsible self is made to understand itself, in a way that remains hidden to the self, as responsible and sovereign without needing a "substantial capacity to act" – a self-relation that is again legitimized by that very philosophical ideal of responsibility (433, 434f.).[33]

---

33 Vogelmann (2014, 433) himself puts it as follows (and I quote this at greater length because this is the point my critique refers to): "Denn indem das Praktikenregime der Philosophie 'Verantwortung' mit höchster Dignität ausstattet – etwa indem 'Verantwortung' zum Definiens des Menschen erklärt wird –, legitimiert es das sich durch Selbstobjektivierung zur Souveränität aufschwingende Selbstverhältnis. Weil dieses jedoch der Fixpunkt all der verschiedenen Gebrauchsweisen des diskursiven Operators Verantwortung ist, überträgt sich die

While Vogelmann's work is a necessary sensitization for the fatal effects of "responsibility", his description of captivity leaves one not only with Honneth's (2014, 15) hint to the costs for the renunciation of responsibility but also with two other doubts: (1) How much is the "captivity" he comes out with in the end due to the claimed unity of different uses of terms of responsibility in the "discursive operator" he starts with (Vogelmann 2014, 23, 124f.)? He uses the notion "operator" and the knowledge about the "uniform structure of the responsible self-relation" (23, 427) the use of this concept has generated[34] as an argument against the objection that the philosophical term "responsibility" is independent of the use of the term in other practices (431). Indeed, the concept of the "operator" makes visible the structural[35] analogies of different uses of responsibility, i.e. the "dealing with the fact of one's subjecting and being subjected" (23). But it also makes less visible – and this might be Vogelmann's own "blind spot" – the differences in content, voluntariness, social context and reputation. To put it more concretely: indeed, there might be structural analogies between the neoliberal use of "Eigenverantwortung" and the responsibility Hans Jonas has written about. But probably due to other differences, the reputation of the latter is not likely to be transferred to the former. (2) Plus, the description of the "captivity" implicitly and axiomatically narrates both the individual and the collective human's potential to resist down – a potential Vogelmann's own plea for a "political fight" will practically rest on.

Responsibility is more ambiguous than Vogelmann's work lets one think. That makes it necessary to differentiate. For this task of (theological) media ethics the substantial work of Vogelmann can be a very helpful sensitization: it highlights that responsibility talk is insofar even in opposition to an orientation to participation as it stabilizes power relations while making them less transparent. It points to the effects of "responsibility" outside theoretical work and to the asymmetries of "responsibility" over against reciprocity orientations. Vogelmann made this plausible for "la-

Legitimation auf alle Praktiken, die sich über 'Verantwortung' selbst explizieren."

34 See: "Die Einheit von 'Verantwortung' findet sich nicht auf der begrifflichen Ebene; nur wenn man 'Verantwortung' als diskursiven Operator in den verschiedenen Praktiken betrachtet, enthüllt sich eine Gemeinsamkeit in all den unterschiedlichen Verwendungsweisen des Wortes Verantwortung" (Vogelmann 2014, 23).

35 Vogelmann (2014, 431f.) names the common structure of the "analyzed uses".

bor" and "philosophy". A public-theological media ethics will have to be sensitive to similar mechanisms in the debates on internet ethics and its own work: What effects does the ethicist's performative attribution of responsibility to others have (see 1.3)? Is the call for a responsible web-2.0 prosumer really emancipative? Does it have a suppressive component insofar as it conceals the subtle power of companies? Where is such a call only the excuse of responsible but overwhelmed legislative and executive institutions?

3 Three suggestions

To conclude: How much am I now responsible for what I do on Facebook to democracy? The discussion of Funiok's work has shown how moral responsibility can plausibly be attributed to individual media users and their associations: as a prosumer of the social web I am – together with politics and enterprises – "co-responsible" for what media communication does to democracy. The recent critiques of responsibility talk point to the ambivalences of responsibility and the problematic effects of its theory: its diffusion could empty the concept, and it can also have disciplinary and disemancipatory dimensions. While the active role of the "prosumer" in web communication makes specific responsibility talk more plausible, it is challenged by the prosumers' lack of professionality and their being manipulated in the "filter bubble".

On the background of these ambivalences of term and situation, I will sketch three short suggestions for how to use "responsibility" in media ethics in accordance with an orientation to participation.

1) Deflation: As reaction to the diffusion of responsibility, which Heidbrink (2003, 48f.[36]) amongst others has diagnosed, he himself suggests the "*contextualistic term 'responsibility'*". The clear criteria of the traditional understanding of responsibility make a "*deflation*" possible, which is also necessary (305, 23) and which does not include disestablishing responsibility as such (49). On the contrary: deflation makes its powerful use possible in the first place (305). Heidbrink develops a concept of responsibility that combines "basic structure and a principal to differentiate" and thereby limits the diffusion and scope of responsibility (51). From Heidbrink (2.1), a theologically informed media ethics shall learn to

36 Vogelmann (2014, 34) is referencing the same term and passage.

attribute responsibility only where the concept allows for it. From Günther (2.2), it can learn to do so only where those made responsible are capable thereof. But if both conditions are given, responsibility should be attributed. As of its scarcity, it is even more meaningful: a person who makes hateful and discriminating posts on Facebook is responsible for that – legally but also ethically – because in doing so one hurts others and contributes to a change of debate culture in a way harmful to the social discourse.

How can people be held responsible in internet communication without establishing a permanent asymmetry in power between those attributing and those holding responsibility (Vogelmann, 2.3)? Mutual attribution in the social web on a horizontal level between media users could be a way: holding one another responsible for what one posts on Facebook and Twitter – with an emphasis on the possible mutuality. This mutuality can be anchored in the history of responsibility as Bayertz (1995) has told it: since being held responsible by one's own conscience was not enough, accountability was conceptualized as a "*public* process", modelled in the concept of "responsible government" (44). Everybody should be accountable to society (44). This corresponds to the "basic thought of an egalitarian democratic society" (44). Fundamental for this is the symmetric mutuality that allows for holding each other responsible: "Jeder Bürger kann für die Folgen seines Handelns von seinen Mitbürgern zur Rede gestellt und zur Verantwortung gezogen werden" (Bayertz 1995, 44).

2) Discourse: Thanks to Vogelmann, the decoupling of imputing and taking responsibility could be seen as problem. Günther pointed to problematic practices of imputing responsibility. Taken together this makes necessary what Günther (2000, 476f.) demands: a social discourse about the presuppositions of attributing responsibility to someone. He puts it more precisely: a discourse about the "implicit concept of personhood" (477). Expanded and applied to media ethics, this could mean that not only a scientific but a social discourse is important about under which condition it is legitimate to attribute responsibility to prosumers and media users.[37] In such a discourse those very prosumers and media users should partake – and they partake already – because such participation prevents from the decoupling Vogelmann pointed to.

3) Holding those in power responsible: According to Bayertz (1995, 36f., 40), the modern ethical concept of responsibility has its roots more in

37 For the necessity of a public discourse about different responsibilities for the public see already Debatin (1998, 125).

political responsibility than in juridical responsibility. In the development of democratic thinking, responsibility was introduced to control the power of the government: the idea of "responsible government" means "that the government [...] is to be accountable to those governed. It is not autonomous but 'responsible'" (37). Hence, originally responsibility was not imputed by the powerful to the powerless but was a terminological means to control those in power. A shift back to this would answer the problems mentioned. Applied to media ethics, this means that media users and prosumers are responsible for what they do, especially for what they publish (Funiok 2011, 179). But they shall also hold responsible those persons and institutions that have influence on the structure of media communication: legislative institutions as well as economical corporations. Funiok has done justice to this because he does not attribute all responsibility only to media users, because the media users are co-responsible for media rules and because he makes controlling media and holding producers responsible a part of the public's responsibility, thus including corporations and their responsibility in his ethics (Funiok 2011, 158f., 119–126, 177; similarly already Debatin 1998, 120f., 123).

It is this aspect in Funiok's ethics that, faced with digitalization and critiques of responsibility, needs to be emphasized: one responsibility of members of the public is to hold those responsible who produce and organize media. In relation to an internet ethics this means: holding fellow prosumers responsible for the content they produce and holding economic corporations and political institutions responsible for the structures of media communication[38]. The responsibility of those in charge needs to be emphasized over against the seduction to overestimate the influence of the public. Faced with digitalization, the focus on virtues of responsible media users is not enough and fails to make participation possible. To be sure, this does not include neglecting the user's responsibility.

To emphasize not only but first of all the responsibility of those in power is also reflected by the further development of TIME's persons of the year. After "we" had been person of the year in 2006, in 2010 it was: Marc Zuckerberg.[39]

---

38 For such discussion on responsibility see also Ingo Dachwitz' summary on https://netzpolitik.org/2016/manipulation-facebook-news-trends/.

39 Cf. http://content.time.com/time/person-of-the-year/2010/.

References

Bayertz, Klaus (1995): Eine kurze Geschichte der Herkunft der Verantwortung, in: Kurt Bayertz (ed.), *Verantwortung. Prinzip oder Problem?*, Darmstadt: Wissenschaftliche Buchgesellschaft, 3–71.

Christians, Clifford G. (1989): Gibt es eine Verantwortung des Publikums? in: Wolfgang Wunden (ed.), *Medien zwischen Markt und Moral. Beiträge zur Medienethik*, Stuttgart: J. F. Steinkopf, 255–266.

Costanza, Christina, Ernst, Christina (2012): Einleitung. Interdisziplinäre Zugänge zu einer Theologie der Social Media, in: Christina Costanza, Christina Ernst. (eds.), *Personen im Web 2.0. Kommunikationswissenschaftliche, ethische und anthropologische Zugänge zu einer Theologie der Social Media* (Edition Ethik Band 11), Göttingen: Edition Ruprecht, 7–15.

Debatin, Bernhard (1998): Verantwortung im Medienhandeln. Medienethische und handlungstheoretische Überlegungen zum Verhältnis von Freiheit und Verantwortung in der Massenkommunikation, in: Wolfgang Wunden (ed.), *Freiheit und Medien* (Beiträge zur Medienethik 4), Frankfurt am Main: Gemeinschaftswerk der Evangelischen Publizistik, 113–130.

Eisel, Stephan (2011): *Internet und Demokratie*, hg. im Auftrag der Konrad-Adenauer-Stiftung e. V., Freiburg im Breisgau: Herder.

Filipović, Alexander (2010): Rezipienten- und Publikumsethik im Web 2.0, Blogeintrag vom 21. Mai 2010, http://www.unbeliebigkeitsraum.de/2010/05/21/rezipienten-und-publikumsethik-im-web-2-0/.

Franzke, Amna (2016): "Die Postredaktionelle Gesellschaft", Interview with Alexander Filipović, *taz* 27/07/2016, http://www.taz.de/!5321764/ (accessed Feb. 2nd, 2017].

Funiok, Rüdiger (1996): Grundfragen einer Publikumsethik, in: Rüdiger Funiok (ed.), *Grundfragen einer Kommunikationsethik*, Konstanz: Ölschläger, 107–122.

Funiok, Rüdiger (2011): *Medienethik. Verantwortung in der Mediengesellschaft* (Kon-Texte), 2nd ed., Stuttgart: W. Kohlhammer.

Greis, Andreas (2001): *Identität, Authentizität und Verantwortung. Die ethischen Herausforderungen der Kommunikation im Internet* (kopaed medienethik 2), München: KoPäd.

Grossman, Lev (2006): You — Yes, You — Are TIME's Person of the Year, http://content.time.com/time/magazine/article/0,9171,1570810,00.html (accessed Feb. 20th, 2017).

Günther, Klaus (2000): Verantwortlichkeit in der Zivilgesellschaft, in: Stefan Müller-Doohm (ed.), *Das Interesse der Vernunft. Rückblicke auf das Werk von Jürgen Habermas seit "Erkenntnis und Interesse"*, Frankfurt am Main: Suhrkamp, 465–485.

Günther, Klaus (2002): Zwischen Ermächtigung und Disziplinierung. Verantwortung im gegenwärtigen Kapitalismus, in: Axel Honneth (ed.), *Befreiung aus der Mündigkeit. Paradoxien des gegenwärtigen Kapitalismus* (Frankfurter Beiträge zur Soziologie und Sozialphilosophie 1), Frankfurt am Main, New York: Campus, 117–139.

Heidbrink, Ludger (2003): *Kritik der Verantwortung. Zu den Grenzen verantwortlichen Handelns in komplexen Kontexten*, Weilerswist: Velbrück Wissenschaft.

Heidbrink, Ludger & Schmidt, Imke (2011): Mehr Verantwortung für den Konsumenten, in: *Ökologisches Wirtschaften*, Nr. 3, 2011, 35–38.

Höhne, Florian (2015): *Einer und alle. Personalisierung in den Medien als Herausforderung für eine Öffentliche Theologie der Kirche* (Öffentliche Theologie 32), Leipzig: Evangelische Verlagsanstalt.

Honneth, Axel (2014): Vorwort, in: Frieder Vogelmann, *Im Bann der Verantwortung* (Frankfurter Beiträge zur Soziologie und Sozialphilosophie 20), Frankfurt am Main, New York: Campus, 9–15.

Jansen, Gregor M. (2003): *Mensch und Medien. Entwurf einer Ethik der Medienrezeption* (Interdisziplinäre Ethik 30), Frankfurt am Main: Peter Lang.

Jarren, Otfried, Donges, Patrick (2006): *Politische Kommunikation in der Mediengesellschaft. Eine Einführung*, 2nd ed., Wiesbaden: VS Verlag für Sozialwissenschaften.

Köhler, Thomas R. (2012): *Der programmierte Mensch. Wie uns Internet und Smartphone manipulieren*, Frankfurt am Main: F.A.Z.-Institut für Management-, Markt- und Medieninformationen.

Lenk, Hans & Maring, Matthias (1995): Wer soll Verantwortung tragen? Probleme der Verantwortungsverteilung in komplexen (soziotechnischen-sozioökonomischen) Systemen, in: Kurt Bayertz (ed.), *Verantwortung. Prinzip oder Problem?* Darmstadt: Wissenschaftliche Buchgesellschaft, 241–286.

Neidhardt, Friedhelm (1994): Öffentlichkeit, Öffentliche Meinung, Soziale Bewegungen, in: Friedhelm Neidhardt (ed.), *Öffentlichkeit, Öffentliche Meinung, Soziale Bewegungen* (Kölner Zeitschrift für Soziologie und Sozialpsychologie. Sonderhefte), Opladen: Westdeutscher Verlag, 7–41.

Pariser, Eli (2012): *Filter Bubble. Wie wir im Internet entmündigt werden*, transl. by Ursula Held, München: Carl Hanser.

Stapf, Ingrid (2006): *Medien-Selbstkontrolle. Ethik und Institutionalisierung*, Konstanz: UVK.

Strohm, Theodor (2000): "Verantwortliche Gesellschaft" – Eine Zukunftsvision ökumenischer Sozialethik? in: *ZEE*, Vol. 44, 203–213.

Veith, Werner (2002): Ethik der Rezeption, in: Thomas Hausmanninger, Thomas Bohrmann (eds.), *Mediale Gewalt. Interdisziplinäre und ethische Perspektiven*, München: Wilhelm Fink, 377–390.

Vogelmann, Frieder (2014): *Im Bann der Verantwortung* (Frankfurter Beiträge zur Soziologie und Sozialphilosophie 20), Frankfurt am Main, New York: Campus.

Wunden, Wolfgang (1996): Auch das Medienpublikum trägt Verantwortung, in: Rüdiger Funiok (ed.), *Grundfragen einer Kommunikationsethik*, Konstanz: Ölschläger, 123–132.

Plain Language as Empowerment beyond a Faithful Middle-class Public:
Contributions of Public Theology to the Capability Approach of Social Justice

Clemens Wustmans

1. Exclusion and theology

Every day we are excluding people from discourses and discussions. I am excluding people, this very text does exclude. Of course I'm not pretending to write or speak the most sophisticated English, but by following certain models of grammar, language style or use of foreign words, I am excluding all those people who can't exert it the same way.

Especially growing up with German as native language, I know about the struggle of others learning German as a foreign language. Yet also for many native speakers it's hard to communicate in a language such as German. Related to this you can observe a very interesting behavior on social media at least in German-speaking contexts: on one side, there is the obvious struggle of many people (and we're talking about native speakers) with German grammar or orthography; on the other side, there's an astonishing number of people feeling being appointed to correct their misspellings, their misuse of foreign words or their incorrect use of grammar. I don't know if it is a typical German issue to adopt the attitude of a teacher and explain to others how to do something right, but I think this behavior impressively shows the clash of different groups within society related to their linguistic capabilities.

Indulging cultural pessimism, you could argue that people become worse and worse educated, leaving school with less and less abilities. But I think a look from the opposite perspective is closer to the truth: there are more people communicating by writing than probably ever before in our history. Thinking for example about my grandparents – my father was the first in family history who was able to go to university, whereas many of his ancestors were farm workers – I don't know anything about their writing skills, because they left nothing written when they passed away. But I know that even in oral discussions they would never have felt to be enabled to discuss for example theological issues; they were "good Christians", they were pious, they "received" what the pastors and the "better educated" said and they made up their mind how to deal with that – but this always remained kind of a one-way communication.

Nevertheless, Karl Barth said, "Theology is not a private reserve of theologians. It is not a private affair of professors. Nor is it a private affair of pastors. Theology is a matter for the church. The term 'laity' is one of the worst in the vocabulary of religion and ought to be banished from Christian conversation." (Barth 1957, 86)

2. Capabilities approach as a postulate of comprehensive inclusion

Speaking of empowerment and capabilities as key elements of participation is well known to debates on social justice. Participation literally means being involved, to participate in something. The term originates from the spheres of justice and economics and was used as generic term for different forms of participation within institutionalized authority groups. An important aspect is the connection with questions of labor; since more and more people in the traditional "industrialized" countries, and even more in countries of the global south, have been excluded because of unemployment, flight and migration or the loss of political and social institutions, an increasing value and importance can be witnessed in the demand of participation and social inclusion. The German Protestant Church (EKD) formulated the core model of the term "Gerechte Teilhabe" – "just participation" – in 2006, which includes a material and an immaterial dimension of participation (Jähnichen 2011, 8). Exclusion means a de facto suspense from society-related or cultural conducts or areas of activity although there are existing equal rights without any legal limitations. Against these tendencies of exclusion a theory of just and equal participation aims at a generalized claim to participate in the chances and opportunities of a society (Kaufmann 1997, 34).

Such an entitled right obtains participation at the basic (common) goods of a society for all parts of the society regardless of gender, religion or ethnical origin and means. These basic goods can be determined as conditional goods because they are the goods that enable people to live an independent and autonomous life. Specifically at a first, access to the basic goods of law and jurisdiction, education, health system and social security are meant. Societies have to provide a certain level of guaranteed entitlements at these goods (Jähnichen 2011, 9). In a theological perspective one can refer towards the universal message of the Christian tradition that includes all people and leads to such a fundamental dimension of justice. The exclusion of individuals or certain groups is in diametrical contradiction against the Christian idea of man and demands an unbending adjustment of such conditions.

A key element of social justice is the capability approach. Capability approach means the political task to create social institutions within the systems of education, health care and social care which enable all citizens of a state to take part at least at the fundamental elements of social life (ibid.). The enabling of a self-responsible and independent living means that the criteria of the capability approach have to be seen as a part of demanded equal opportunities, because very different individuals are facing very different starting conditions for their participation at public life. According to that, social justice means the elementary removal of social discriminations to enable all members of the society to face equal chances and similar conditions of living. Access at a responsible participation in social life is the aim.

The reduction of social injustice and inequality as a key focus of the capability approach leads towards an orientation at the theological norm of the option for the poor, weak and disadvantaged. They need special support and empowerment to equalize and compensate disadvantages in a special way. To provide appropriate institutions of education has to be the related demand.

Discussing the question of how public space is constituted, German sociologist Martina Löw notices that space is more than the physical container that surrounds us; it is shaped and designed by people while participating in this very space. According to Löw, the opportunities of setting up space are depending on symbolical and material factors found in the specific action situation. This includes the habitus of the person, structural organized inclusion or exclusion and not just physical capabilities. Space creates distribution, which, for a hierarchical society, mostly means: uneven distribution, distribution that favors certain groups (Löw 2015, 272). I as a theologian think we have to ask ourselves if it is consistent to the concept of public theology that such exclusions are accepted as "natural". Does this comply with the demand of social justice that we expect from so many other actors of society?

You can talk of social justice in different perspectives: in its meaning related to common good and public welfare or as a particular form of justice. This second option aims at social balance by instruments of distributive justice. It is its ethical concern to approve the right of participation as a human right and to embed this politically – in opposite to the liberal idea of the state as a coordinator of a just formal freedom. Wolfgang Huber designs a model of justice of public goods, including four aspects:

- fairness of the conditions of contracts and exchange between individual persons and groups;
- equal opportunities for active participation;
- distributive justice as a way to create and sustain social balance (including the option for the poor as a priority);
- legal justice in the execution of legal practice (Huber 2006).

Especially the biblical reasons and foundations of the option for the poor are showing the special meaning of social aspects for a Christian-based ethics talking about justice. It is understood as the care for inter-human joint relationships as the answer to the faithful covenant loyalty of God. It can be identified by its mutual respect and compassion; its foundation is laid in the connection of justice and mercy (Bedford-Strohm 1993, 150ff.).

The second aspect Huber mentions has to be highlighted in particular in this case: equal opportunities for active participation have to include the use of language accessible not just to a well-educated middle class. The option for the poor cannot be limited to economic issues but has to be applied to public discourses in democratic societies – and in debates of public theology, at least, if we take it seriously talking about "public". If this public is not just a faithful middle-class public, educated and used to a specific vocabulary, the inclusion of broader parts of Christianity has to be the aim. And as long as language skills are such a main factor of exclusion, plain language could be an instrument to think about.

You can find similar thoughts in newer philosophical theories of justice. Especially Martha Nussbaum and Amartya Sen are highlighting the importance of concrete, specific living conditions as foundation and the opportunities to improve them. They both do measure societies on the protection and the chances to participate offered to their members. Sen emphasizes that different people – who, in a Christian-based anthropology, are sharing the same dignity – are in need of very uneven amounts of abilities before they can participate. Instead of declaring abstract human beings as a standard, thus being similar in their concerns to their dignity and their capabilities, he takes the perspective of those who are threatened in their dignity and rights because of less fortunate conditions (Sen 2009, 303).

3. Plain language as element of the capability approach

One important aspect of an inclusive, accessible organization of society is the use of plain language: writing designed to ensure the reader understands as quickly, easily and completely as possible. The UN Convention on the Rights of Persons with Disabilities includes plain language as one of the "modes, means and formats of communication" (UN Convention 2006).

Representatives for plain language often present Cicero as early advocate for plain language: "When you wish to instruct, be brief; that men's minds take in quickly what you say, learn its lesson, and retain it faithfully. Every word that is unnecessary only pours over the side of a brimming mind." (Cicero 2004, 58) Cicero argues that the plain style is not easy. While it may seem close to everyday speech, achieving the effect in formal discourse is a high and difficult art: "Plainness of style seems easy to imitate at first thought, but when attempted, nothing is more difficult" (ibid.). The modern history of analyzing and implementing plain language began in the United States' movement towards plain English in the 1940s.

The chosen vocabulary must remain simple and familiar. Everyday language should be favored against acronyms, jargon and legal language. Plain language favors the use of the verb form of the word instead of the noun form. To enhance clarity, plain language privileges the active voice, in which the subject does the action of the verb. Sentences written in plain language have a positive construction and address the reader directly.

Writing in plain language also takes into account the presentation of the text. It is important to choose a font that is easy to read, setting it to an adequate size. Sentences written in capital letters are harder to read because the letters are less distinguishable from one another. Simple design elements like leaving white spaces, using bullets and choosing contrasting colors encourage a user to read the text and make it easier to read.

To give an easy example of plain language: Instead of "Firearm relinquishment is a mandatory condition" one would write, "You must hand over your guns." – "High-quality learning environments are a necessary precondition for facilitation and enhancement of the ongoing learning process" would be replaced by "Children need good schools if they are to learn properly."

However, theology as a part of the "humanities community" emphasizes specific and specialist language as a central tool and condition of its work. Elaborate language often seems the key for the rating and valuation of theological contributions. These thoughts correspond to the tractates of

Ludwig Wittgenstein and his postulate that philosophical problems can only be understood or dissolved by someone who understands by which misapplication of language they are generated at all.

The core of Wittgenstein's early philosophy is the linguistic theory of language. Afterwards, reality is divided into "things" (things that are related to one another). Each "thing" has a "name" in the language. The meaning of these names is given by their cohesion in the sentence. Sentences decay in their names like reality decays in things. If the arrangement of names in the sign of a sentence has the same structure as the arrangement of the objects represented by the names in reality, thus representing the same "state of affairs", a sentence becomes true. If things are really different from their names in the punctuation mark, a proposition becomes wrong (Wittgenstein 1921).

Wittgenstein's ideas which lead to the linguistic turn – "the limits of my speech are the limits of my world" – are an important counterargument against efforts to simplify theological language. On the other hand, it has to be emphasized that, especially from a protestant perspective, it seems to be at least irritating if the aspect of making theology accessible via the language used by "ordinary people" is questioned: it was a core concern of Martin Luther and the protagonists of the reformation, commemorated this year all over the world, to translate biblical scriptures instead of reading out Latin texts during service. A withdrawal on complex language, as educated as possible, excluding large parts of the community, seems to be the opposite of the efforts of the reformation. Promising efforts in this very field can be found at the public of the church: "Baden-Wurttemberg reads Luther" is the name of the campaign of the Evangelical church in Württemberg and Baden organized for 2017. It focuses on Luther's work "Von der Freiheit eines Christenmenschen". The new edition of this pamphlet invites an update to the most important thoughts of the reformer. It contains the text, which is also offered in excerpts in a translation in plain language. Here we have a low-threshold offer to discover reformist freedom (Kohler-Weiss 2016).

Talking about language and the world opened through it, one is led to another area of theories: to Jürgen Habermas and the complex of the public sphere which leads directly towards the core of what public theology aims for. The public sphere is an area in social life where individuals can come together to freely discuss and identify societal problems and, through that discussion, influence political action. Hauser has defined it as "a discursive space in which individuals and groups associate to discuss matters of mutual interest and, where possible, to reach a common judgment about them" (Hauser 1999, 61). The public sphere can be seen as "a theater in modern societies in which political participation is enacted through the medium of talk" (Fraser 1992, 57) and "a realm of social life in which public opinion can be formed" (Asen 1999, 42).

Describing the emergence of the public sphere in the 18th century, Jürgen Habermas noted that the public realm, or sphere, originally was "coextensive with public authority", while "the private sphere comprised civil society in the narrower sense, that is to say, the realm of commodity exchange and of social labor" (Habermas 1989, 30). Whereas the "sphere of public authority" dealt with the state, or realm of the police, and the ruling class (ibid.), the "authentic 'public sphere'", in a political sense, arose at that time from within the private realm, specifically, in connection with literary activities, the world of letters (ibid., 30–31). This new public sphere spanned the public and the private realms, and "through the vehicle of public opinion it put the state in touch with the needs of society" (ibid., 31). "This area is conceptually distinct from the state: it [is] a site for the production and circulation of discourses that can in principle be critical of the state." (Fraser 1992, 57) The public sphere "is also distinct from the official economy; it is not an arena of market relations but rather one of discursive relations, a theater for debating and deliberating rather than for buying and selling" (ibid.). These distinctions between "state apparatuses, economic markets, and democratic associations [...] are essential to democratic theory" (ibid.). The people themselves came to see the public sphere as a regulatory institution against the authority of the state (Habermas 1989, 27). The study of the public sphere centers on the idea of participatory democracy and how public opinion becomes political action.

The basic ideal belief in public sphere theory is that the government's laws and policies should be steered by the public sphere, and that the only legitimate governments are those that listen to the public sphere (Benhabib 1992, 75). "Democratic governance rests on the capacity of and opportunity for citizens to engage in enlightened debate." (Hauser 1998, 83) Much of the debate over the public sphere involves what is the basic theoretical structure of the public sphere, how information is deliberated in the public sphere and what influence the public sphere has over society.

The basic discourse of the theory of Habermas is the distinction between communicative action (the act of speaking) and a strictly "strategic approach", as developed in the theory of communicative action. According to this understanding, strategic action is parasitic to communicative action, which is the original mode of speech. In communicative action, a speaker regularly raises validity claims, which, depending on the statement, appear to be the (propositional) truth, the (normative) correctness and the (subjective) truthfulness and aim at the consent of his counterpart. If this goal is missed, no agreement is reached; this is the point of departure for the discourse, which is problematized by the claims of validity, which are raised on the one hand and criticized on the other, functioning "as a body of appeal for communicative action" (Habermas 1995, 130).

In his theory of communicative action, Jürgen Habermas calls discourse a process of negotiating individual claims of individual actors (also referred to as "actuators" in Habermas). According to Habermas, a characteristic of language is the inherent rationality. The results of a communication – if it is free of distortions by power or hierarchies – are, according to him, necessarily rational. As an ideal, as the best assurance of true knowledge, he sees the "rule-free discourse", built on discourse norms (basic equality of the participants, theoretically problematizability of all topics and opinions, theoretically uncloseness of the audience) and authentic feelings. The resulting communicative reality is supposed to bring the best argument to profit – which can be further developed (Link & Link-Heer 1983, 88).

In conclusion it has to be asked: If theology demands social justice and capabilities to participate for those who are facing worse conditions and if the *one* instrument that leads to participation in the theological discourse is language – how can theology and especially *public theology* demand (such a demand, with all its struggles and challenges, e.g., expressed in Huber 1993, 9–12) to include *the* public. It could lead to the impression that the sphere of the private people is gathered to be the audience instead of the community.

4. Public theology – which public?

It has to be asked if public theology (at least in its academic manifestation) addresses just certain parts of public with a specific social background and education who already are involved in the reflection of public debates and political deliberation. Accepting plain language matching the reading skills of a larger audience could be a chance to widen the intended public in democratic societies.

To compare the ability of building language skills to, for example, the access to some attractive living space in an attractive urban neighborhood does show the accordance: you need material goods and resources, often a well working social networking or even a specific rank in society

(Wüthrich 2013, 12). To participate in social discourses it's almost the same – language skills are the gatekeeper, and they are built within the same social conditions and restrictions. While it is at least intellectually obvious for members of universities or academic institutions that the buildings we're working in, where we're doing research and teaching, are designed to give access even for all those colleagues, students or guests dependent to a wheelchair, the large group of people who cannot afford educated language skills is excluded. This is not just accepted but even defended.

Writing in plain language does not mean oversimplifying the concepts but presenting the information in a way that makes it easier to understand and use by a wider audience. Texts written in plain language are still formal, but they are easier to read and inspire confidence for the reader. Another aspect: Using plain language in communications ultimately improves efficiency, because there is less ambiguity for the readers and less time is taken for clarifications and explanations. If you'd like to argue a bit nasty against theologians – perhaps "less time for clarifications and explanation" is not exactly what we want to reach for. But the defensive arguments should have been taken serious. The connection between the communication of complex thoughts and theologies on the one hand and the use of a complex system of languagc on the other cannot be denied. A reduction of the linguistic expression can't deny a reduction of content, which cannot be the aim of a theological discourse.

At first glance there seems to be a matching concept in other disciplines of science and humanities: public understanding of science / public communication of science. It is a comparatively new approach to the task of exploring the multitude of relations and linkages science, technology and innovation have among the general public. While earlier work in the discipline had focused on augmenting public knowledge of scientific topics, in line with the information-deficit model of science communication, the discrediting of the model has led to an increased emphasis on how the public chooses to use scientific knowledge and on the development of interfaces to mediate between expert and lay understandings of an issue.

But criticism expressed towards this corresponding concept of "public understanding of science" has been taken serious also in the context of public theology. Public communication of science may explicitly exist to connect experts with the rest of society, but its very existence can be understood as an act of strengthening the border: the impression given may then be one of a condescending scientific community inviting the public to "play" but not to discuss issues in earnest. Efforts how to avoid such effects have to be fundamental for public theology.

5. Remaining tensions

The scholarly debate on public engagement with science developed further into analyzing the deliberations on science through various institutional forms, with the help of the theory of deliberative democracy. Public deliberation of, and participation in, science practiced through public spheres became a major emphasis. It is argued for wider public deliberation on science in democratic societies which is a basic condition for decision making regarding science. There are also attempts to develop more inclusive participatory models of technological governance in the form of consensus conferences, citizen juries, extended peer reviews and deliberative mapping. And should these examples from the area of science and technology match not even more as we are talking about public theology?

It can be summed up that an area of tension remains: all those who are excluded from my contribution because of their language capabilities are individuals with an own undetachable dignity. They are a part of exactly the public that should be addressed by public theology. Especially the example of the capability approach through the use of plain language shows us how challenging it remains to think of participation as important aspect of social justice. A condescending, patronizing way of widening the discourse has to be avoided; instead of talking to some less educated and skilled audience from a superior position, the idea of a community has to be focused – with all its challenges, difficulties and tensions.

References

Asen, Robert (1999): Toward a Normative Conception of Difference in Public Deliberation, *Argumentation and Advocacy*, Vol. 35, No. 3, 115–129.

Barth, Karl (1957): *Theologische Fragen und Antworten*, Zollikon.

Bedford-Strohm, Heinrich (1993): *Vorrang für die Armen. Auf dem Weg zu einer theologischen Theorie der Gerechtigkeit*, Gütersloh: Kaiser.

Benhabib, Seyla (1992): Models of Public Space, in: Craig Calhoun (ed.), *Habermas and the Public Sphere*, Cambridge, Mass.: MIT, 73–98.

Cicero (2004): *Orator*, ed. by Harald Merklin, Stuttgart: Reclam.

Fraser, Nancy (1992): Rethinking the Public Sphere. A Contribution to the Critique of Actually Existing Democracy, in: Craig Calhoun (ed.), *Habermas and the Public Sphere*, Cambridge, Mass.: MIT, 109–142.

Habermas, Jürgen (1989): *The Structural Transformation of the Public Sphere. An Inquiry into a Category of Bourgeois Society*, Cambridge, Mass.: MIT (Translation from the original German, published 1962).

Habermas, Jürgen (1995): Wahrheitstheorien (1972), in: Jürgen Habermas, *Vorstudien und Ergänzungen zur Theorie des kommunikativen Handelns*, Frankfurt am Main: Suhrkamp, 127–186.

Hauser, Gerard A. (1999): *Vernacular Voices. The Rhetoric of Publics and Public Spheres*, Columbia: University of South Carolina Press.

Huber, Wolfgang (1993): Vorwort, in: Rasmus C. Birch, Larry L. Rasmussen: *Bibel und Ethik im christlichen Leben*, Gütersloh: Kaiser, 9–12.

Huber, Wolfgang ([3]2006): *Gerechtigkeit und Recht. Grundlinien christlicher Rechtsethik*, Gütersloh: Gütersloher Verlagshaus.

Jähnichen, Traugott (2011): Teilhabegerechtigkeit als sozialethisches Leitbild. Gegen die zunehmende Ungleichheit in der postindustriellen Arbeitsgesellschaft, *Amos International*, No. 2, 2011, 5–11.

Kaufmann, Franz-Xaver (1997): *Herausforderungen des Sozialstaats*, Frankfurt am Main.

Kohler-Weiss, Christiane (ed.) (2016): *Von der Freiheit. Martin Luther lesen. Mit Auszügen in Leichter Sprache*, Gütersloh: Gütersloher Verlagshaus.

Link, Jürgen, Link-Heer, Ursula (1983): *Elementare Literatur und generative Diskursanalyse*, München: Fink.

Löw, Martina ([8]2015): *Raumsoziologie*, Frankfurt am Main: Suhrkamp.

Sen, Amartya (2009): *The Idea of Justice*, London: Lane.

UN Convention on the Rights of Persons with Disabilities (2006), https://www.un.org/development/desa/ disabilities /convention-on-the-rights-of-persons-with-disabilities.html.

Wüthrich, Matthias (2013): Eine raumtheoretische Skizze der Voraussetzungen und ihrer Relationierung, *Ethik und Gesellschaft*, No. 1, 2013: *Der "spatial turn" der sozialen Gerechtigkeit*, http://www.ethik-und-gesellschaft.de/mm/EuG-1-2013_ Wuethrich.pdf, 5–16.

Theology and Public Democratic Institutions:
Public Theology in the Context of the German and Swiss National Ethics Councils

Christine Schliesser

Introduction

Recent developments in established democracies both in Europe and North America have presented challenges to democracy that seemed hardly feasible even a few years ago. The rapid rise of right-wing radical parties throughout Europe – including European "core countries" such as Germany and France –, the endeavors of a democratically elected government in countries like Turkey to turn this nation into an authoritarian presidential system or the emergence of "alternative facts" and "post facts" as widely accepted in the current democratically elected US government are met with increasing concern both within and outside of Europe. These developments necessitate a (re)turn to the most fundamental questions of democracy. What exactly do we mean by "democracy", the "rule of the people"? And who can claim to be "the people"? And, since a pluralism of religions and *weltanschauung* is a constitutive element of Western democracies, what is the role of religion and theology, respectively, as the scientific reflection on religion, in democratic processes?

According to political scientist Larry Diamond, democracy is a system of government characterized by the following four elements: *first*, the choice and replacement of the government through free and fair elections; *second*, the active participation of the people as citizens in the spheres of politics and civil society; *third*, the protection of human rights of all citizens; *fourth*, a rule of law that applies equally to all citizens (Diamond 2004, 2016). In this contribution, the focus will be on the second key element of democracy, the participation of citizens. The national ethics councils of Germany and Switzerland, a specific institutionalized means of citizen participation in democratic processes, serve as the framework to situate our main research questions: What is the role of religion – and, more specifically, of public theology – in these public democratic institutions? And what is the specific contribution of public theology to democratic processes, in these councils and beyond?

Three steps will serve to explore possible answers to these questions. In a *first* step, I will introduce the national ethics councils of Germany and Switzerland and delineate their place within the democratic process and democracy's discursive practices of the formation of opinion as well as of moral and legal norms. The focus will be on the political function of these councils in parliamentary democracies. After this theoretical groundwork, in a *second* step I will turn to the *de facto* role of theology in these specific public democratic institutions. I base my observations on an extensive empirical study I conducted between 2013 and 2016, including qualitative interviews with theological and non-theological representatives within Germany's and Switzerland's national ethics councils. Here, significant differences regarding the role of theology between the German and the Swiss ethics councils will emerge. A *third* and final part seeks to draw out the specific resources and contributions of public theology in public democratic institutions – and beyond. Drawing on the theological tradition of the *munus triplex*, the three-fold office of Jesus Christ, I will make the case for a Christologically centered public theology as a productive and indispensable voice in a pluralistic democratic society.

1. Public democratic institutions: The political function of national ethics councils. The examples of the German Ethics Council (DER) and the Swiss National Ethics Councils (EKAH and NEK)[1]

When Germany and Switzerland established their national ethics councils in 2001/2007 (NER/DER),[2] 1998 (EKAH) and 2001 (NEK), they were following an international trend to institutionalize public ethical discourse. National ethics councils are located at the intersection of the spheres of the political and civil society. Accordingly, their tasks comprise two main areas, political consulting and informing the wider public on ethical issues.

---

1 German Ethics Council/*Deutscher Ethikrat* (DER) (http://www.ethikrat.org/), *Eidgenössische Ethikkommission für die Biotechnologie im Außerhumanbereich* (EKAH) (http://www.ekah.admin.ch/en/homepage/), *Nationale Ethikkommission im Bereich der Humanmedizin* (NEK) (http://www.nek-cne.ch/en/homepage/).

2 In 2001, Germany's National Ethics Council (*Nationaler Ethikrat*, NER) was founded. After much criticism concerning its legal foundations based on a decision of the federal government instead of a parliamentary decision, the NER was replaced by the DER in 2007.

Political consulting includes the preparation of opinions and recommendations for political and legislative action, while the councils' public activities are directed at informing the public, encouraging discussion in society and engaging the various social groups. Usually, the cooperation with other national ethics councils as a third task is desired as well. The scope of Germany's DER is comparatively wide, including "questions of ethics, society, science, medicine and law that arise and the probable consequences for the individual and society that result in connection with research and development, in particular in the field of the life sciences and their application to humanity" (EthRG 2,1). The national ethics councils of Switzerland, on the other hand, divide their workload into questions arising from biotechnology with regards to human beings (NEK) and issues related to non-human biotechnology (EKAH).

While the tasks of national ethics councils are specified in their respective legal documents, their *political function* in parliamentary democracies still remains somewhat unclear. Political scientist Gordian Ezazi points to three possible theoretical interpretative patterns of their political function, namely discourse ethics, theory of power and micro politics (Ezazi 2016, 17–51). A discourse-ethical interpretation can be based on Alasdair MacIntyre's observation that ethical discourse in modern democratic societies is largely characterized by "interminableness" and "disagreement" (MacIntyre 1984, 6). The increasing institutionalization of public ethical discourse is therefore also understood as the attempt to help solve ethical problems through formalized and institutionalized procedures (cf. Schockenhoff 2005, 404).

From the perspective of power theory, the relationship between politics and science/scientists is of fundamental concern. Relying on Michel Foucault's analysis of power (Foucault 2013, 257ff.), this interpretation views ethics councils as a means of stabilizing and supporting the existing power structures of the political class. From a theological perspective, this line of interpretation is taken up by Eilert Herms, who critiques the "staging of public ethical discourse on the level of committees" as "instruments of a campaign to generate acceptance" of already formed decisions (Herms 2009, 63).[3]

The micro-political interpretation is based on a conflict-sociological heuristics that understands conflicts of value in politics as being framed as ethical questions. The result is, according to sociologist Alexander

3 Translations CS, if not indicated otherwise.

Bogner, an "ethicization" (*Ethisierung*) of biopolitical issues (Bogner 2009). Opinions published by national ethics councils and mirroring different ethical perspectives on a certain subject serve therefore less as an argumentation base for politicians but rather as a signal that a free decision of conscience is required.

This brief overview already shows that the political function of national ethics councils in deliberative democracies is far from clear-cut. Rather, this issue itself is part of the on-going critical and self-reflective process within these councils. In its public plenary meeting on September 22nd, 2016, on "Ethics Consulting and Public Responsibility" (*Ethikberatung und öffentliche Verantwortung*), for instance, the DER reflected on its own self-understanding and its role in politics and civil society. Again, different perspectives surfaced (cf. Infobrief 01/17, 6f.).

In his empirical study of the DER, Ezazi arrives at a similar conclusion, namely that the normative self-understanding of members with regards to the political function of the DER is multi-facetted. Nevertheless, most perspectives can be structured along the two poles of either "politization", focusing on the DER's political consulting tasks, or "ethicization", aiming at the ethical information of both politicians and civil society by including a wide range of different ethical arguments (Ezazi 2016, 235). Instead of *the* (one and only) political function of national ethics councils, we therefore need to speak of their political *functions*. The ambiguity regarding the political function of national ethics councils is mirrored by unclarity concerning the reception and impact of the council's opinions on the side of the parliamentarians. Furthermore, a mediating authority between council and parliament is missing; institutions such as the German Parliamentary Advisory Board on Ethics (*Parlamentarischer Ethikbeirat*) failed because its political mandate lacked definition. Another aspect that needs mentioning here refers to the appointment procedures of the councils' members. While the 12 members of the EKAH and the 15 members of the NEK are elected by the seven federal councilors, the DER's 26 members are appointed by the President of the German Parliament, half on the proposal of the Parliament and half on the proposal of the Federal Government. All terms are four years, with a maximum of three terms in the Swiss councils[4] and of two terms in the DER. Both the German and the Swiss coun-

4 While the *Verordnung über die nationale Ethikkommission im Bereich der Humanmedizin* (VNEK 2.7) restricts members to three terms, there is no equivalent legal specification for the terms of the EKAH members.

cils would benefit from an increased transparency in the nomination and appointment processes.

To sum up, the discussion of the political function of national ethics councils in parliamentary democracies has resulted in a rather diverse picture of different possible functions that both academic discourse and council members themselves attribute to these councils. Of the issues emerging from this result, the following two seem to be of particular significance. *First*, the interdisciplinary and scientific study of national ethics councils requires further investment in the development of a national ethics councils' theory. Such a theory could help to clarify the councils' political role(s) in parliamentary democracies as well as to identify (possibly unwarranted) expectations connected to these institutions. Critical and self-reflective discussions within the councils themselves constitute an indispensable part of this process. *Second*, this result necessitates a stronger focus on the individual council members, whose normative self-understanding of the political function of their council significantly impacts the outlook and output of their respective council. As the discussion so far has shown, it is less a certain theoretical framework that shapes the concrete work of a national ethics council but rather their individual members. This holds true not only with regards to the political function of national ethics councils but for the role of theology in these councils as well. To this we will turn now.

2. *On the role of (public) theology in Germany's and Switzerland's national ethics councils*

The German and the Swiss national ethics councils are characterized by a plurality of disciplines and ethical perspectives according to their respective legal foundations. Contrary to the Swiss councils, however, the German Ethics Council Act explicitly calls for the inclusion of theological representatives (EthRG 4,1). Nevertheless, theologians are also present in both the EKAH and the NEK, if not by legal right, but by customary right and the stakeholder principle. While all three councils include both a Protestant and a Catholic university theologian, the DER again stands out due to the fact that it additionally includes one representative of each the Protestant and the Catholic Church. This is met with astonishment, even resistance in the Swiss councils. As Alberto Bondolfi, Catholic theologian in the NEK (2001–2013) states, "we shook our heads when we saw that there are bishops in the DER. To us, such a thing is unthinkable, absolutely unthinkable."[5]

Bondolfi's reaction already indicates that there are significant differences between the role of theology and the role of the churches in the Swiss and in the German national ethics councils. First, however, some explications regarding the terminology of the "role" are necessary. Role is employed here in a generic sense which means that it does include the possibility of several different roles that can be assumed by theology in these councils. Furthermore, according to Trutz Rendtorff, it is the double-sidedness of the sociological concept of the role that accounts for its productivity (Rendtorff 2004, 381). On the one side, there is the self-perception of theology and its representatives; on the other side, there is the outer perception of theology as well as expectations, for instance, by the state and civil society. In order to gain a clearer perception of the *de facto* role of (public) theology in the DER, EKAH and the NER, we therefore need to listen to the self-understanding of its representatives and to its reception by non-theological members.

The results of my empirical study of the German and Swiss national ethics councils reveal two significant discrepancies, one pointing to the differences between the role of theology in these two neighboring democracies and the other indicating a tension between the self-perception of theological representatives and their perception from the outside. The first finding can be illustrated by two statements, by Johannes Fischer, Protestant theologian in the Swiss NEK (2001–2007), and by Wolfgang Huber, Protestant theologian in the German DER (2010–2014). Fischer states, "I never understood myself in such a way as if I was representing theology or the church there [sc. in the NEK], possibly even with the intent to endow these with more influence there. I was there as Johannes Fischer, who comes up with his own thoughts." Emphasizing the fact that he understood himself exclusively as a private individual in the NEK, Fischer refutes any "insinuation" that his presence might be due to his representation of his discipline, theology, or his church. In line with his self-understanding, Fischer declares that theology in the form of "theological reasons or arguments" does not play any role in the NEK. Quite contrary to Fischer, Huber – former bishop of the Protestant Church in Germany – emphasizes that theology is present in the DER and does indeed play a

---

5 For the full transcripts of the interviews conducted please contact the author at christine.schliesser@sozethik.uzh.ch.

role, also in the form of "theological language" that he himself employs. Huber characterizes his own self-understanding as representing "responsible freedom" (*verantwortete Freiheit*) that he derives from the Gospel's message of freedom. As a theologian, Huber says, one also needs to "overtly assert" one's place in the intellectual debate.

These heterogeneous impressions are mirrored by other interview partners in the respective councils. Klaus Peter Rippe, philosopher and president of the Swiss EKAH (2000–2011 and since 2016), points out that in his perception, the theologians present in the EKAH strive to "factor out their own theology" (*das eigene Theologische ausklammern*). Anton Losinger, Catholic auxiliary bishop in the DER (2008–2016), on the other hand, sees a clear role of theology in his council. He illustrates this role by pointing to the "strong minority opinions" initiated by the theologians present there. Eberhard Schockenhoff, Catholic theologian in the DER (2008–2016), supports Losinger's self-perception as belonging to a "minority". To him, the role of theology is further characterized by the "capability to resist" (*Resistenzfähigkeit*) the majority and to call into question existing plausibilities.

The emerging picture of theology playing a far more visible role in the German national ethics council as compared to its Swiss counterparts can be framed in culture-hermeneutical terms as well. In Switzerland, freedom of religion is traditionally interpreted in terms of freedom *from* religion. The public role of the churches in Switzerland assumes therefore a strongly civil-religious connotation, as Thomas Schlag points out (Schlag 2014, 86). In his *History of Switzerland*, Volker Reinhardt observes how the Helvetic "art of mediation and agreement" (Reinhardt 2007, 119) runs through the Swiss culture and also infuses Swiss theological and church landscapes. Dissenting or even confrontative voices are therefore more likely to be regarded as threats to consensus-building attempts than as unique and productive contributions in their own rights. On the level of national councils, both Swiss and German members refer to the more amiable dimension of the Swiss communication culture, even though Losinger stresses that the atmosphere in the DER is less confrontative and "aggressive" than in its predecessor institution, the NER.

All theologians in the DER emphasize their self-understanding as theologians and claim a visible role of theology for their council. This self-perception, however, stands in a certain tension with the outside perspective, leading us to the second observed discrepancy mentioned above. According to Volker Gerhardt, philosopher in the DER (2008–2012), "theological ethics as theological does not exist" in the DER. This observation is supported by Christiane Woopen (2008–2016), medical ethicist and President of the DER (2012–2016). She detects a certain theological "background murmur" (*Hintergrundrauschen*) that is not being made explicit. Only "if one knows of the theological dimensions, then one can comprehend what position or ethical argument is likely to be theologically grounded." Asked for her understanding of the tasks of theology in the DER, Woopen points to several concrete *desiderata*. She asks that "theology or theological ethics develop a clearer profile *as* theological ethics. Why not say that you are viewing a certain issue from this or that specific foundational or justificatory horizon? There is no reason not to do so." Woopen proposes that theologians could include specific theological arguments in the DER's published opinions by marking the line that separates generally intelligible reasoning from horizons that reach beyond. She cautions, however, that such a procedure might also be received with a certain resistance. "This will not only meet with friendly reactions, this is entirely clear … yet I expect from the theological representatives that they still act accordingly, because this is their actual contour." Woopen further demands of the theologians the integration of explicitly Christian terminology such as love or the perspective of the good, besides the perspective of the right. She continues, "and what I am clearly missing empirically is the perspective of a horizon of meaning" (*Perspektive des Sinnhorizontes*), i.e. to make clear "why it is good to do something in a certain manner, because it gives a deeper meaning to life."

The contrast between the outside perspective and the self-perception of the DER's theologians is heightened once we focus on one particular theological paradigm, public theology. Huber, member of the DER and doyen of German-speaking public theology, understands it as the quest to "interpret the questions of communal life and its institutional forms in their theological relevance and to ask for the contribution of the Christian faith to the responsible design of our life-world" (Huber 1996, 14), which in our context includes the question regarding the contribution of the Christian faith to democracy. Heinrich Bedford-Strohm, also one of public theology's currently most renowned protagonists in Germany, adds that public theology has a "clear theological profile" (Bedford-Strohm 2016, 10). He proposes five criteria to help define public theology (Bedford-Strohm 2009, 53). Public theology is, *first*, engaged in issues of public relevance, *second*, bilingual, *third*, 'glocal' by combining contextuality and universality, *fourth*, interdisciplinary, and *fifth*, interested in the theological-ethical reflection of concrete political issues. In his interview, Huber emphasizes his engagement in public issues and the need for an interdisciplinary approach. Different from Bedford-Strohm, however, Huber speaks of translation instead of bilingualism.[6] In view of public theology's self-understanding as promoting a "clear theological profile", its tension with the outside perspective as "background murmur" seems quite remarkable. As one possible explanation one might point to the different concepts of theology that seem to be engaged here. Huber's concept of theology and theological ethics as "responsible freedom" might be quite different from the one employed by Gerhardt or Woopen, thereby leading to the differences in the perception of theology's role. Nevertheless, a certain tension remains as (public) theology's lack of profile observed by Woopen and Gerhardt in the DER is echoed by Lucius Kratzert's critique of public theology as "lacking contour" (Kratzert 2015, 13). Yet if the profile of public theology remains unclear, its specific contribution to public democratic institutions as well as to democracy in general remains vague as well. This problem seems to be partly rooted in the fact that while public theology is not short of formal characteristics – as the ones named by Bedford-Strohm –, there are only few criteria of content that could give shape and profile to public theology. This links to the question of a "Public Dogmatics" (Harasta 2013). In the final part, I would therefore like to propose a Christologically oriented understanding of public theology as a productive way to lend shape and profile to it in public democratic institutions such as national ethics councils and beyond.

3. Contributions of public theology to democracy: Why public theology needs a Christological orientation

Public theology serves pluralistic democratic societies by providing research and expertise with regards to the relationship of *weltanschauungen* to the public sphere. Yet it goes beyond the mere descriptive. As Wolfgang Vögele points out, public theology both reflects the effects of Christianity in the public spheres and understands itself as constituting an active part of these effects (Vögele 1994, 421f.). Yet how can public theology take an active part in democratic processes? What are its tasks? Answers

6 While the concept of translation refers to the transformation of theological language into secular accessible language, bilingualism presupposes translational processes, yet goes beyond them. Different from translation that results in a new monolingualism, namely the secular accessible language, bilingualism strives for the continuing presence of both languages, theological and secular, in communication processes.

to these questions need to keep in mind public theology's core characteristics, namely being "public" and being "theology". It must neither give in to liberal demands striving to relegate religion to the mere private realm nor confuse theology with politics.

In my own quest for tentative answers, I rely on Michael Welker's proposal to utilize the traditional dogmatic figure of the *munus triplex* to explicate more clearly the contributions of public theology to democracy, while at the same time serving a Christologically oriented profile of public theology (Welker 2013). According to Welker, public theology faces four main tasks (Welker 2013, 282–285). *First*, public theology needs a thorough sociologically grounded analysis of our societies.[7] Based on a sociologically informed understanding, we need, *second*, a "*hermeneutics of personal and interpersonal communication*" in order to "consciously and systemically influence the power circulation of our societies" (Welker 2013, 283). *Third*, public theology must identify concrete issues, problems and concerns. Each of the three tasks described must be accompanied by the *fourth* level, on which "we have to deal with God's revelation and God's sustaining, rescuing, saving and ennobling work and guidance" (Welker 2013, 285). In order to do justice to these four tasks, public theology is, according to Welker, dependent on a Christological orientation. The teaching of the *munus triplex*, the three-fold office of Christ as king, prophet and priest, proves to be of particular productivity in this regard, not least due to the fact that it constitutes, as Edmund Schlink observes, a unique ecumenical phenomenon as it is accepted in different confessional traditions (Schlink 1983, 414). Christ's three offices allow us to gain a deeper understanding of the "*public Christ*" (Welker 2013, 286) in life's different dimensions.

With respect to the kingly office of Christ, the ethical implications of Christ's pre-Easterly life come into sharper focus. His practice of egalitarian table-fellowship, of love and forgiveness, mutual care, inclusion and respect are characteristics of a king who is at the same time the friend of the poor and marginalized. Welker sees here a "constant movement towards radical democracy" (Welker 2013, 287). In the discipleship of Christ, public theology is called to give shape to the kingdom of God in its political, social and cultural implications for this life. Examples are found in the efforts aimed at mandatory education and health-care access in

---

7 One example is the utilization of milieu theory for theological thinking and practice, for instance, with regards to baptism (cf. Hempelmann et al. 2013).

many societies. "What a great orientation for any public theology!" (Welker 2013, 287) On the level of national ethics councils this orientation might take shape by the integration of Woopen's proposal to include a terminology of love. The care for the poor and marginalized as represented in the kingly office of Christ can be exemplified in the vicarious concern for those that are underrepresented even in democracies. This is illustrated by Losinger, for instance, when he points to the advocatory function of theological representatives in discussions on the beginning or end of life. One could further deliberate how it is possible to (better) include the people affected by the respective discussions in the councils in a respectful manner. Duncan Forrester's motto "We must never talk about the poor behind their back" springs to mind here (cf. Storrar 2007, 18).

Christ's prophetic office points us to the cross that not only witnesses to the most dramatic situation of the *conditio humana* but at the same time, through the resurrection, constitutes the turning-point in the world and in its salvation. "In the light and darkness of the cross of Christ, the prophetic office gains its shape and its depth" (Welker 2013, 288f.). While the cross of Christ does refer us to the utter hopelessness of humankind, at the same time it reminds us of the hope that Christ brings. Public theology is therefore always a theology of hope. From this follows, according to Welker, the critical and self-critical search for truth and justice. In its prophetic dimension, public theology is called to cry out against injustice. In this, it seeks the cooperation with secular partners in the academic and legal systems, in civil societies and education, as it makes full use of the resources provided by democracies. "Again, what a great challenge and task for a global public theology!" (Welker 2013, 289) In view of the participation of (public) theology in public ethical discourse, the prophetic office of Christ refers us to both the critical and self-critical function of theology. In the awareness of its own fallibility and limits, theology can be a fearless witness to truth and justice. Schockenhoff illustrates this dimension by emphasizing the necessity to "be critical towards societal plausibilities" and to cultivate – next to the capacity to dialogue – a "certain capability to resist". Woopen's comment is in a similar vein when she demands a clearer profile of theologians in the DER, even if this will not only meet with friendly reactions.

Christ's priestly office ought to be unfolded in the light of the resurrection, as Welker suggests. The early church expressed the testimony of the resurrection in a variety of symbolic actions such as the breaking of bread, the greeting of peace and the reading of Scripture. The Lord's Supper further shows the interrelatedness of Christ's three offices. Next to the priestly office, the kingly office and Jesus Christ's merciful care for people become just as apparent in the celebration of the Lord's Supper as the prophetic office and the distressing memory of Christ's suffering. The priestly office "witnesses to God's will that the humans constitute not only symbolic table-fellowship but also a community of mutual acceptance, mutual care, of justice and peace. […] It reveals a God who shows his mercy not only by healing and restituting human life, but rather by elevating and ennobling it" (Welker 2013, 290). In view of Christ's priestly office, Welker notices a particular relationship between public theology and the (public) church. "With the priestly office, the definitely ecclesial responsibilities and loyalties of public theology come into view" (Welker 2013, 290). How, then, can Christ's priestly office as a dimension of public theology gain shape in concrete democratic contexts such as national ethics councils? Certainly, one needs to beware of attempting to "ecclesialize" pluralistic and public democratic institutions. Nevertheless, even in interdisciplinary ethics committees public theology keeps in mind the inherent relationship between church and theology, which Rendtorff expresses as the "irrefutable relatedness" (*unabweisbar aufeinander bezogen*) of church and theology (Rendtorff 2004, 395).[8] The explicit detachment of theological members from their own church (and discipline) as seen in Fischer or Bondolfi can therefore hardly be reconciled with our conception of theology and church as inherently connected.

It is thus the interplay of all three of Christ's offices as king, prophet and priest that can serve public theology as an inspiration and orientation not least in the public democratic arena.[9] A Christologically grounded and oriented public theology will be clearly audible as a distinct theological contribution within the choir of interdisciplinary and pluralistic voices in national ethics councils and beyond. Yet how can the voice of public theology not only be audible but also intelligible? This is ensured by its ad-

8 In a paradigmatic way, Friedrich D. E. Schleiermacher describes the relationship between theology as a positive science and the church by emphasizing that theology is directed towards the practical task of church leadership (Schleiermacher 2002, § 1, 139f.).

9 Furthermore, the threat of public theology's fragmentation through the diverse theological and societal contexts united under the "umbrella paradigm" of public theology is reduced due to a common Christological center. This danger was already noticed by Linell Cady, "The diversity of issues potentially connected with the notion of public theology threatens to overwhelm the concept" (Cady 1991, 108).

herence to bilingualism, that is by speaking in such a way that employs both theological as well as secular accessible language games. By means of its Christological foundation as explicated in the figure of Christ's threefold office, public theology's indispensable contributions in matters of public relevance become apparent, not in order to seek a privileged position of Christianity in society but in order to serve a common good in pluralistic, democratic societies. As John de Gruchy states, "Public theology as Christian witness does not seek to preference Christianity but to witness to values that we believe are important for the common good" (de Gruchy 2007, 30).

References

Bedford-Strohm, Heinrich (2009): Politik und Religion. Öffentliche Theologie, *VF*, Vol. 54, 42–55.

Bedford-Strohm, Heinrich (2016): Fromm und politisch. Warum die evangelische Kirche die Öffentliche Theologie braucht, *Zeitzeichen*, Vol. 17, No. 7, 8–11.

Bogner, Alexander (2009): Ethisierung und die Marginalisierung der Ethik. Zur Mikropolitik des Wissens in Ethikräten, in: *SozW*, Vol. 60, 119–137.

Cady, Linell E. (1991): H. Richard Niebuhr and the Task of a Public Theology, in: Ronald F. Thiemann (ed.), *The Legacy of H. Richard Niebuhr*, Minneapolis: Fortress Press, 107–129.

de Gruchy, John W. (2007): Public Theology as Christian Witness. Exploring the Genre, in: *IJPTh*, Vol. 1, 26–41.

Deutscher Ethikrat (DER)/German Ethics Council, http://www.ethikrat.org/ (accessed Feb. 20th, 2017).

Diamond, Larry (2004): *What is Democracy?*, Lecture at Hilla University for Humanistic Studies, 21/01/2004, http://web.stanford.edu/~ldiamond/iraq/WhaIsDemocracy 012004.htm (accessed Feb. 20th, 2017).

Diamond, Larry, Morlino, Leonardo (2016): The quality of democracy, in: Larry Diamond (ed.), *In Search of Democracy*, London: Routledge, 33–45.

Eidgenössische Ethikkommission für die Biotechnologie im Außerhumanbereich (EKAH)/Federal Ethics Committee on Non-Human Biotechnology, http://www.ekah.admin.ch/en/homepage/ (accessed Feb. 20th, 2017).

Ethikratgesetz/Ethics Council Act (EthRG), http://www.ethikrat.org/about-us/ethics-council-act (accessed Feb. 20th, 2017).

Ezazi, Gordian (2016): *Ethikräte in der Politik. Genese, Selbstverständnis und Arbeitsweise des Deutschen Ethikrates*, Wiesbaden: Springer.

Foucault, Michel (2013): *Analytik der Macht*, ed. by D. Defert, F. Ewald, Frankfurt am Main: Suhrkamp.

Harasta, Eva (2013): Glocal Proclamation? An Excursion into "Public Dogmatics" Inspired by Jürgen Moltmann and Heinrich Bedford-Strohm, in: Heinrich Bedford-Strohm, Florian Höhne, Tobias Reitmeier (eds.), *Contextuality and Intercontextuality in Public Theology. Proceedings from the Bamberg Conference, 23.–25.06.2011*, Berlin: Lit, 291–299.

Hempelmann, Heinzpeter et al. (2013): *Handbuch Taufe. Impulse für eine milieusensible Taufpraxis*, Neukirchen-Vluyn: Neukirchener Verlagshaus.

Herms, Eilert (2009): Die Bedeutung der Weltanschauungen für die ethische Urteilsbildung, in: Friederike Nüssel (ed.), *Theologische Ethik der Gegenwart. Ein Überblick über zentrale Ansätze und Themen*, Tübingen: Mohr Siebeck, 49–71.

Huber, Wolfgang (1994): Öffentliche Kirche und plurale Öffentlichkeiten, in: *EvTh*, Vol. 54, 157–180.

Huber, Wolfgang (1996): *Gerechtigkeit und Recht. Grundlinien christlicher Rechtsethik*, Gütersloh: Gütersloher Verlagshaus.

Infobrief 01/17, http://www.ethikrat.org/dateien/pdf/infobrief-01-17.pdf (accessed Feb. 20th, 2017).

Kratzert, L. (2015): Einblick ohne Überblick, *RefPr*, Vol. 47, 13.

MacIntyre, Alasdair (1984): *After Virtue. A Study in Moral Theory*, 2nd ed., Notre Dame, Ind.: University of Notre Dame Press.

Nationale Ethikkommission im Bereich der Humanmedizin (NEK)/National Advisory Commission on Biomedical Ethics NCE, http://www.nek-cne.ch/en/homepage/ (accessed Feb. 20th, 2017).

Reinhardt, Volker (2007): *Geschichte der Schweiz*, 2nd ed., München: C. H. Beck.

Rendtorff, Trutz (2004): Die Autorität der Freiheit. Theologische Beobachtungen zur öffentlichen Rolle der Evangelischen Kirche in Deutschland, in: *ZThK*, Vol. 101, 379–396.

Schlag, Thomas (2014): Reformierte Kirche im helvetischen Kulturkontext. Deutsch-Schweizerische und deutschschweizerische Perspektiven, in: Birgit Weyel, Peter Bubmann (eds.), *Kirchentheorie. Praktisch-theologische Perspektiven auf die Kirche*, Leipzig: Evangelische Verlagsanstalt, 80–93.

Schleiermacher, Friedrich Daniel Ernst (2002): *Kurze Darstellung des theologischen Studiums zum Behuf einleitender Vorlesungen (1811/30)*, ed. by D. Schmid, Berlin: de Gruyter.

Schlink, Edmund (1983): *Ökumenische Dogmatik: Grundzüge*, Göttingen: Vandenhoeck & Ruprecht.

Schockenhoff, Eberhard (2005): Plattform gesellschaftlichen Dialogs. Braucht es Bischöfe und Theologen im Nationalen Ethikrat?, in: *HerKorr*, Vol. 59, 403–406.

Storrar, William (2007): A Kairos Moment for Public Theology, in: *IJPTh*, Vol. 1, 5–25.

Verordnung über die nationale Ethikkommission im Bereich der Humanmedizin (VNEK), http://www.nek-cne.ch/fileadmin/nek-cne-dateien/Dokumentation/Rechtliche_Grundlagen/VNEK.pdf (accessed Feb. 20th, 2017).

Vögele, Wolfgang (1994): *Zivilreligion in der Bundesrepublik Deutschland*, Gütersloh: Gütersloher Verlagshaus.

Welker, Michael (2013): Global Public Theology and Christology, in: Heinrich Bedford-Strohm, Florian Höhne, Tobias Reitmeier (eds.), *Contextuality and Intercontextuality. Proceedings from the Bamberg 23.–25.06.2011*, Berlin: Lit, 281–290.

The Public Role of the Church in the Democratic Society: The Lutheran World Federation's Document "The Church in the Public Space" as an Inspiration for Public Theology

Eva Harasta, Berlin

1. Introduction

Heinrich Bedford-Strohm's definition of public theology as liberation theology for a democratic society is a product of its German context as well as a normative claim for this same context (Bedford-Strohm 2009, 176). Presupposing a functioning, well-defined mutual relationship between the church(es) and state institutions, Bedford-Strohm's approach emphasizes that academic theology and the churches mostly support the state's endeavors for more social justice. They also monitor the political arena on behalf of the marginalized, thus carrying out liberation theology's central tenet, the preferential option for the poor. Still, with its trust in the state and in big intermediary institutions as agents for justice, this interpretation of public theology may strike some readers from outside of Germany as a rather surprising form of *liberation* theology. Liberation theology, after all, brings to mind a grass-roots movement with deeply critical views of the state and of "the powers that be"; liberation theology takes an active part in social struggles and may even carry a taste of revolution at times. Does public theology turn liberation theology on its head by developing it into an officially sanctioned, cooperative state theology? Understood in this way, this German approach would represent an appropriation of liberation theology, using the strong legacy and high esteem of liberation theology in global ecumenical contexts for the purposes of an establishment theology and establishment church. But what place does liberation theology have at the table of the powerful?

The response to this critique hinges on the second part of Bedford-Strohm's definition: public theology is liberation theology *for a democratic society*. In a democratic society, the power lies with the electorate, with the people. As such, sitting at the table of the powerful in a democratic society means sharing one's bread with as many different parts of society as possible. In contrast to traditional liberation theology approaches from the global South that presuppose a strong opposition to "the state", the circumstances of a functioning democracy offer more cooperative ways of political theology. In a democratic society, the struggle to make the voice of the marginalized heard in the public discourse takes on a different form – as it can take its cue from the established rights of the marginalized as members of the electorate. Ideally, the preferential option for the poor here simply needs to remind the democratic state of its duties rather than accuse it of injustice and systematic disenfranchisement. Within the framework of Bedford-Strohm's public theology, this also applies to the preferential option for the globally marginalized: public theology needs to raise its voice for global economic justice as well, advocating in the context of first world democracies for more justice in the global economy.

This last aspect touches upon the inherently inter-contextual character of public theology.[1] For even as public theology shares with liberation theology a deeply contextual concern (speaking to the public of its given time and place about social justice for the people who share this concrete context), its very ambiance, the ever open and fluid "public", puts it in the midst of a wide variety of interconnecting economic, political, social, religious, media, and academic influences. Accordingly, the public theology community places a strong emphasis on exchange, both within its own context and with other contexts. The Global Network for Public Theology (GNPT, founded in 2007) plays a key role in fostering such exchange in the realm of academic theology.[2] In the realm of public theology with regard to inter-contextual church relations, the Lutheran World Federation (LWF) is starting to play a key role. In the following, I will introduce the LWF's public theology study document because I am convinced that the academic public theology discourse may profit greatly from exchange with public theology endeavors within the churches – and especially from exchange with the LWF. Academic public theology as it is alive in the GNPT (and in the Berlin Institute for Public Theology) shares a deep interest in inter-contextual and intercultural exchange, in social advocacy, and in developing theological reflection on the public role and witness of the church in the wider context of society. At least from a German perspective, any rigid separation of the academic public theology discourse

1 On the inter-contextual character of public theology, cf. this volume of articles: Bedford-Strohm et al. (2013).

2 This is the moment to acknowledge that this paper was first presented at the GNPT consultation «Democracy and Social Justice in Glocal Contexts" in Stellenbosch, South Africa, October 2016. The author is thankful for questions and comments she received there.

and the churchly public theology discourse seems strange. After all, Heinrich Bedford-Strohm, the leading voice within German public theology, combines a background in academic public theology with church leadership in his roles as Bishop of the Lutheran Church in Bavaria (since 2011) and Chairman of the Council of the EKD (since 2014). Academic public theology has much to profit from and to contribute to the reflection on the public responsibility of the church(es).[3]

The Lutheran World Federation has been preparing for the big anniversary in 2017 with several theological study processes and ecumenical initiatives; these endeavors are the context of its public theology activities. Among the ecumenical initiatives, the reconciliation process between Lutherans and Mennonites and the dialogue process with the Roman Catholic Church about the reformation anniversary are maybe the most high profile endeavors. One very visible fruit of the ecumenical labors of the LWF was the joint Lutheran and Roman Catholic worship service on October 31, 2016, in Lund. While the preparations for the anniversary in Germany focused mainly on discussing the protestant identity and educating the general public about Protestantism, the LWF opened the anniversary year with a common worship service in the cathedral of Lund held by Antje Jackelén, the Archbishop of the Church of Sweden, and Pope Francis. However, more to the point, in addition to these initiatives regarding external relations, the LWF is in the process of reflecting on major theological issues. Three issues were chosen as seminal for the immediate future of the LWF: biblical hermeneutics, the LWF's self-understanding as a communion of churches, and, thirdly, the public role of the church, i.e., public theology.

The public theology study group worked on the study process from 2014 to 2016. Its seven members were chosen from all regions of the LWF, and Dr Antje Jackelén, Archbishop of the Lutheran Church of Sweden, chaired the study process.[4] In June 2016, the LWF council approved

---

3 Such exchange also conforms with public theology's "bilinguality", a term that was coined by Heinrich Bedford-Strohm, refering to the two languages of public theology: its explicitly theological language and its participation in the language of public reason (as inspired by Habermas). For my view on the problem of public theology's bilinguality, see: Harasta (2009).

4 The members of the group were Bishop em. Dr Suneel Bhanu Busi (India), Dr Eneida Jacobsen (Brazil), Dr Kathryn M. Lohre (USA), Rev. Lusungu Mbilinyi (Tanzania), Dr Jerzy Sojka (Poland), and the author of this article. Rev. Dr Simone Sinn, study secretary of the department of theology at the

the study document "The Church in the Public Space"; a short statement was also issued to facilitate easy access for a broader church public. Accordingly, the paper may rightfully claim quite a high profile as an official document of the Council of the Lutheran World Federation. Yet as a study document, it is intended to be re-interpreted and further developed. Only the reception process of the document will show whether the Lutheran member churches also see a *kairos* for public theology.

2. The LWF study document "The Church in the Public Space"

This second part of my paper serves to summarize the study document. The document draws on the Lutheran tradition in order to give reasons for engaging in the public discourse, and it suggests which challenges are of special importance for the churches' public witness. In order to achieve this, the argument takes five steps.

(1) The first step is clarifying the notion of "public space". After quite some discussion, the study group decided to take a normative approach, delineating what kind of public space should be the aim of the churches' activities instead of describing deficient forms of public life (e.g. dynamics of exclusion in Southern India or instances when a church failed to give public witness) or summarizing a specific contextual approach to public space (e.g. Jürgen Habermas' idea of public reason or David Tracy's threefold understanding of theological publicness). Rather, the paper offered three basic principles to define a *just* public space: safety for the marginalized, meaningful participation of all groups in society, and equal access to common goods and to political decision-making processes. (LWF 2016, 16)[5]

(2) The second step in the paper's argument focuses on the theological underpinnings of the church's role in the public space. The first draft of the paper put the emphasis on Christian freedom and on the distinction be-

LWF headquarters in Geneva, coordinated the group meetings and the editing of the study document. Two additional LWF staff members also participated in the process: Rev. Dr Kenneth Mtata (Zimbabwe, study secretary for biblical hermeneutics) and Dr Ojot Ojulu (Ethiopia, a member of the LWF's advocacy department). The group members are listed in: LWF (2016), 39.

5 However, a trace of Tracy remained as it was stressed that these principles not only apply to the public of civil society in general but also to the public space within the church.

tween the two realms of God's rule. But in the course of the study process, it became clear that these ethical aspects needed to be supplemented by doctrinal aspects in order to portray the (desired) interconnection between the church's ethical advocacy work and its spiritual life more adequately. Thus, baptism and the Lord's Supper were named as the *foundation* of the church's public role, in the sense that baptism is a vocation to live in faith, love and hope, and in the sense that the Holy Communion strengthens Christians in their day-to-day life. Yet baptism and Eucharist were of course also differentiated from the public witness of the church as they only include church members. They are not themselves "public witness" but its basis. (LWF 2016, 19)

Only *after* this reference to the sacraments, the paper introduces the Lutheran distinction between the two realms of God's rule as a steppingstone for approaching the church's public role. The two-realms concept has deeply influenced Lutheran interpretations of the state's authority and the church's role alongside the state. For a German perspective, the controversies in the Confessing Church about the "two-realms doctrine" remain a poignant warning, as they contributed to an "a-political" view of the church and to appeasement policies in relation to the NS regime. Yet in spite of such misuses, the distinction between the two realms of God's rule remains relevant for today's public witness of Lutheran churches: "[I]t helps us to understand how we can interact with people outside the church in the public arena without insisting they become Christian. [...] In this way, it provides an orientation for living the Christian vocation in a religiously plural society. A further strength of this concept lies in its diagnostic power in reference to the complex interaction between religion and politics."(LWF 2016, 20) This diagnostic power of the concept helps to guard against "the politicization of religion and the 'religionization' of politics" (LWF 2016, 21), which of course is one of the most important challenges facing the public role of religion today.

(3) After reflecting on the notion of public space itself and offering theological underpinnings for accepting that the church does indeed carry a public responsibility, the paper takes a third step by describing guiding principles for the public role of the church itself. These three guiding principles are faith, hope, and love.

The principle of *sola fide* – necessarily combined with *sola gratia* as it refers to justification faith – reminds the church that it depends wholly and fully on God's grace, in its ethical public witness as much as in the internal spiritual discourse. Acknowledging this dependency helps define the specific authority with which the church acts in the public realm: the church cannot claim any superior position in the sense of a "holy authority"; rather, it shares with all of creation a deep dependency on God's grace, being not only affected but also participating in actively perpetuating social injustices. (LWF 2016, 23)

The principle of *hope* reminds the church of the universal scope of God's justice and grace. This helps encourage a broad reach of the church's public work, because it urges to look beyond one's given context. An active interest in transcending regional, cultural, ideological boundaries is fundamental for the church's public role. Additionally, hope points towards the need of creating new public spaces, and it leads into imaginative ways of engaging with the public and in public. Hope calls for broadening the horizon of the church whenever possible. (LWF 2016, 24)

The third guiding principle for the church's public role is neighborly *love*, which here refers to the preferential option for the marginalized. At first glance, this may seem like a non-democratic guideline: "The Christian witness in the public space is not directed by the math of the most influential majorities but by the quest for God's justice and grace for all."(LWF 2016, 25) Yet this principle seeks to guard against "blind" or "self-evident" majorities and aims at including as many voices as possible in the public decision-making process, reaching compromise and consensus by negotiation, and building sustainable majorities – which is of course a deeply democratic way of going about things. By the third principle, the public role of the church is described as fundamentally dialogical, that is, open to the demands of others while drawing on its view of a just place for all, and open to ever changing constellations of "center" and "margins".[6]

The three principles for delineating the public role of the church are thoroughly theological as they are meant to inspire the self-understanding of the church in the public space. The tools of working towards a just public space for all, however, need to be accessible to non-Lutheran approaches. Regarding such tools, the paper points to human rights. (LWF 2016, 37)[7]

6 The distinction between center and margins is in itself part of the dynamic of marginalization. So the study document used this distinction cautiously: "[T]he church is called to reevaluate cultural distinctions between center and margin, between powerful and oppressed, between low and high." (LWF 2016, 37). Accordingly, the paper stresses that "[t]he proper place for the Lutheran public witness is both at the center and at the margins of society." (25)

7 This notion ties in with public theology's "bilinguality" (see above note 3).

(4) After reflecting on the notion of public space, offering theological underpinnings for Lutheran public engagement and describing guiding principles for the church's public role, the paper takes the fourth step: pointing out central challenges for public engagement on the local, regional and global levels. Five areas were named: engagement for refugees, engagement for gender justice, engagement for climate justice, engagement for peaceful interreligious relations, and engagement for overcoming exclusion. When viewed from an academic public theology perspective, the naming of these five challenges can be understood as a request for advice. Concise theological arguments and multi-faceted interdisciplinary forms of thoughts are much needed in order to reach effective and sustainable forms of public work on the part of the churches. Academic public theology has the resources to respond. Yet translating these resources for the broader church audience in a constructive, well-informed and relatable manner does represent a challenge for academic public theology. It is a promising challenge, though. After all, how could public theology ever claim to be publicly relevant if it failed to convince the churches and their members, who are of course part of the general public?

(5) The fifth and final step of the paper gives five suggestions on methods for churchly engagement in the public space, naming an "ABCDE" of the Church's Engagement in the Public Space. The ABCDE is: *Assessing* public issues in participatory ways, *Building* relationships of trust, *Challenging* injustice, *Discovering* signs of hope and *Empowering* people in need. (LWF 2016, 33–34)

3. *Conclusion: Thinking about the public role of the church in a democratic society*

In conclusion, I offer three remarks that discuss the LWF paper from an academic public theology perspective, and then I offer three further – and more general – remarks on the interaction between academic public theology and "the churches". All six remarks may be understood as thoughts on possible future avenues for the Berlin Institute for Public Theology if the reader is thus inclined.

- First, three remarks regarding the LWF paper itself:

(1) The LWF paper offers a normative approach to "the public space". It does not describe or investigate different publics. Even including empirical investigations of the different contexts represented by the seven members of the study group would have made the aim of the paper – a globally

translatable inspiration for public engagement – hard or even impossible to reach, as it would have led into a swarm of details, while simultaneously opening the dilemma of justifying the exclusion of other contexts. Additionally, one can make a case for ascribing the task of investigating a specific context to the churches that are part of that context themselves. – Yet the normative character of the LWF paper also testifies to the focus on ethics that is prevalent in academic public theology so far. Interdisciplinary exchange with practical theology promises to be propitious for overcoming this empirical blind spot.

(2) The paper tries to connect its ethical trajectory with elements from the Lutheran doctrinal tradition. In a sense, it offers a kind of (Lutheran) "public ecclesiology" in a nutshell. This invites reflection on the possibility of (Lutheran) public theology dogmatics. Placing doctrinal thought under the condition of showing the relation of doctrinal topics to the public role and action of the church promises to be both a new challenge and an inspiration for dogmatic thinking. Yet envisioning a unity of ethics and doctrine under the auspices of describing the public witness and relevance of the church admittedly is a quite ambitious project.

(3) The LWF paper is intended for a wide variety of recipients: individual Lutherans, local congregations, regional churches, church communions on a regional level and finally the global church communion of the LWF itself. Whether it succeeds in reaching these diverse recipients remains to be seen. Still, the broad and varied horizon of the LWF paper may inspire public theology to think more thoroughly about its intended audience, and to try reaching diverse strata of the public discourse.

- Second, three remarks regarding the interaction between academic public theology and "the churches":

(1) A hermeneutical aspect: What is the difference between doing public theology in the context of a global communion of churches and doing public theology in the context of a global network of research institutions? The LWF paper presupposes that there is a common ground between Lutherans anywhere in the world, be they in Brazil, in Austria or in Hong Kong. The common ground is the shared Lutheran denomination. In comparison, academic public theology (within the Global Network for Public Theology) is both more diverse and more homogeneous. It is more diverse because the participating research institutes have backgrounds in different denominations. But the GNPT is, in a sense, also much more homogeneous than the LWF, because its core group is composed of academic theologians who are involved in theological ethics, and who are part of a global elite with the means of meeting regularly in different places (such as

Princeton or Stellenbosch). How could more diversity and an exchange with different rationalities be accomplished without sacrificing academic standards?

(2) A doctrinal aspect: In what way is public theology denominational? Maybe it is a typically Lutheran perspective to ask this question. However, an emphasis on contextuality is a basic trait of public theology – and the denominational background certainly is an important part of any theologian's context. So far, such denominational aspects are made explicit only occasionally in public theology contributions. Further reflection on denominational differences may be a part of the inter-contextual endeavors of public theology (in the GNPT). I pose this as an ecumenical question, but one might imagine it as an inter-religious question as well. (Should we try to get into contact with public theology institutes from other religious traditions?)

(3) A structural aspect: Theological departments in global ecumenical or denominational institutions could be interesting dialogue partners in future public theology – on the very basis of acknowledging that research and church policy are two different issues that can inspire each other.

References

Bedford-Strohm, Heinrich (2009): Vorrang für die Armen. Öffentliche Theologie als Befreiungstheologie einer demokratischen Gesellschaft, in: Friederike Nüssel (ed.), *Theologische Ethik der Gegenwart. Ein Überblick über zentrale Ansätze und Themen*, Tübingen: Mohr Siebeck, 167–182.

Bedford-Strohm, Heinrich, Höhne, Florian, Reitmeier, Tobias (ed.) (2013): Contextuality and Intercontextuality in Public Theology: Proceedings from the Bamberg Conference 23.–25.06.2011, *Theology in the Public Square*, Vol. 4, Berlin, Muenster, Wien, Zuerich: LIT.

Harasta, Eva (2009): Karl Barth, a Public Theologian? The One Word and Theological 'Bilinguality', in: *International Journal of Public Theology*, Vol. 3, No. 2, 184–199.

LWF (2016): *The Church in the Public Space: A Study Document of the Lutheran World Federation*, Geneva.

Authors

Prof. Dr. Andreas Feldtkeller teaches Comparative Religion and World-wide Christianity at the Faculty of Theology, Humboldt-Universität zu Berlin.

PD Dr. Eva Harasta is Director of Studies for Theology and Inter-Religious Dialogue at the Evangelical Academy Berlin.

Dr. Florian Höhne is research associate and assistant lecturer at the chair for Systematic Theology (Ethics and Hermeneutics) at the Humboldt-Universität zu Berlin.

Prof. Dr. Mouez Khalfaoui is a Senior Professor of Islamic Jurisprudence and Islamic Thought at the University of Tübingen.

Prof. Dr. Torsten Meireis teaches Ethics and Hermeneutics at the Faculty of Theology, Humboldt-Universität zu Berlin. He serves as founding Director of the Berlin Institute for Public Theology.

Prof. Dr. Matthias Möhring-Hesse is Professor for Theological Ethics / Social Ethics at the Catholic-Theological Faculty of the Eberhard Karls Universität Tübingen.

Prof. Dr. Marcia Pally teaches Multilingual Multicultural Studies at New York University, at Fordham University, and is a regular Guest Professor in the Faculty of Theology, Humboldt-Universität zu Berlin.

Prof. Dr. Rolf Schieder holds the chair of Practical Theology and Religious Education in the Faculty of Theology at the Humboldt-Universität zu Berlin. He is chairman of the Program on Religion and Politics and serves as Vice-Director of the Berlin Institute for Public Theology.

Dr. Christine Schliesser is Associate Researcher at the Institute for Social Ethics of Zurich University's Center for Ethics.

Dr. Clemens Wustmans is research associate and assistant lecturer at the chair for Systematic Theology (Ethics and Hermeneutics) at the Humboldt-Universität zu Berlin.